PERFECT PHRASES in

German

for Confident Travel

The No *Faux-Pas* Phrasebook
for the Perfect Trip

Hyde Flippo

New York   Chicago   San Francisco   Lisbon   London   Madrid   Mexico City
Milan   New Delhi   San Juan   Seoul   Singapore   Sydney   Toronto

1 2 3 4 5 6 7 8 9 10 11 12 13 14 15 16 17 18 19 20 FGR/FGR   0 9

ISBN   978-0-07-149989-7
MHID   0-07-149989-X

McGraw-Hill books are available at special quantity discounts to use as premiums and sales promotions or for use in corporate training programs. To contact a representative, please e-mail us at bulksales@mcgraw-hill.com.

This book is printed on acid-free paper.

Contents

Contents

Introduction

Unlike the typical phrasebook, *Perfect Phrases in German for Confident Travel* treats the cultural aspect of the language as an essential element. Not only will you be able to communicate at a basic level in German, but you'll also know when and why to say what you want to say. Speaking German (or any language) involves much more than mere words or grammar. *Perfect Phrases* will give you the fundamental cultural awareness and knowledge of daily life that can help you communicate more effectively, get things done, and avoid cultural embarrassment.

In each theme-based section of this phrasebook you'll find essential phrases along with cultural information that goes hand-in-hand with those phrases. Although the primary focus of this book is Germany, it can be used in all three of the main German-speaking countries: Austria, Germany, and Switzerland.

German-speakers appreciate it when visitors make the effort to speak their language. Be assured that they don't expect perfection, and they will forgive any minor mistakes you might make. But *Perfect Phrases in German for Confident Travel* is designed to help you avoid many potential faux pas, both when using the language and when immersed in the culture.

The phrases within this book are grouped into major themes that include dining out, driving, accommodations, money matters, shopping, talking about the weather, and many other activities. Each phrase has an English translation and a phonetic guide to help you pronounce the German correctly. Each chapter contains useful sentences and expressions designed to make your trip easier and more enjoyable. The main phrases at the beginning of each section within the chapters are frequently followed by detailed cultural insights explaining their context. Those entries are then usually followed by extra German phrases that will greatly improve your ability to communicate and converse.

We hope you will enjoy using *Perfect Phrases in German for Confident Travel* and that it will not only help make your journey more fun but will also give you a better, deeper understanding of life in German-speaking Europe.

Gute Reise!   Have a good trip!
GOO-tuh RYE-zuh

Pronunciation Guide

In addition to an English translation, each entry provides a phonetic representation of the German pronunciation designed so that you will feel confident speaking in German. Simply pronounce the syllables in the phonetic guide as they would be said in English. Most of these phonetic representations are self-explanatory, but this guide will clarify some elements of German pronunciation that differ from English.

First, an important point about German spelling and German pronunciation in general: Unlike English, German spelling is very consistent, and once you learn the way the spelling and sounds match, you can pronounce German words you've never seen before. Some examples:

- The **ei** spelling in German is always pronounced like the English word *eye*.
- The opposite **ie** spelling always sounds like the *ee* in *feel*. (No "*i* before *e* except after *c*"!)
- The German **eu** spelling always sounds like the *oy* in *toy*.
- The German **w** is almost always pronounced like an English *v*.

The few exceptions to these rules are usually found in words borrowed from English or French.

Most consonants are pronounced similarly in German and English, although the German **r** is crisper and shorter (not rolling on as in American English). Some other consonant exceptions to keep in mind are:

- The consonants **b** and **d** have a different sound when they are at the end of a word in German. The **b** sounds like an English *p*, while the German **d** has a *t* sound at the end of a word.
- The English *th* sound (as in *the*) does not exist in German; **th** in German sounds the same as a **t**.
- The German **ß** letter (called an *ess-tsett*) sounds like a double-**s** (**ss**). Recent German spelling reform has changed some German words that were formerly spelled with an **ß** to an **ss** spelling: **daß/dass** (*that*), **Kuß/Kuss** (*kiss*). But the **ß** is still used in many common German words: **Straße** (*street*). The **ß** is not used at all in Swiss German.
- The German **sch** spelling at the front of a word or syllable is always pronounced like the English *sh*.
- The sound of the German **sp** or **st** spelling at the front of a word or syllable is shown in the guide as **shp** or **sht**.

The pronunciation of vowels and diphthongs (two vowels combined, like the *oy* in *boy*) can be very different in German and English. In order to use the phonetic representations in this book to their full advantage, follow these guides for vowel sounds. The letters in bold represent what you will see in the phonetic representations.

- **ah** is pronounced like the *a* in *father*
- **ay** is pronounced like the *ay* in *say*
- **ee** is pronounced like the *ee* in *eel*

- **ow** (German **au**) is pronounced like the *ow* in *how* or *now* (never as in *tow* or *throw*)
- **oy** (German **eu** or **äu**) is pronounced like the *oy* in *boy* or *toy*

The umlauted vowels **ä**, **ö**, and **ü** have unique sounds in German that do not exist in English. Using English, it is not really possible to duplicate their true pronunciation in German. Our guide offers only an approximation as follows:

- for **ä**, **ay** represents the sound as in the *ay* in *say*
- for **ö**, **er** represents the sound as in the *er* in *fern*
- for **ü**, **ew** represents the sound as in the *u* in *lure*, but pronounced with pursed lips

The phonetic representation **kh** stands for the German **ch** sound at the end or near the end of some German words. It sounds somewhat like an English *k*, but is softer, with air continuing to flow over the tongue, very similar to the *ch* sound in the Scottish word *loch*.

Remember as you use this book, however, that you don't need to have a perfect German pronunciation to be understood, and that German-speakers will appreciate your efforts to speak their language.

Chapter 1

Good Manners

 Guten Tag! *(GOO-ten tahk)*: Hello!

This is the standard, everyday greeting in most of Germany. Since it literally means "good day," this form of hello is used from morning until night. In the morning you can also say *Guten Morgen!* In the late afternoon, evening, or after dark, you would say *Guten Abend!* (There is no phrase for "good afternoon" in German.) A new trend in Germany, particularly in the north, is to say *Hallo!*, a word once used mostly to get someone's attention (like "Hey!"), but now used just like the English word "hello." (See the following sections for greetings used in Austria and Switzerland.) Today in Germany, in informal situations, you may also hear *Hi!*—borrowed from English and used mostly by the younger generation. Although you may hear it, it is better not to use *Hi!* yourself, since it could be interpreted as being too familiar.

The way you say hello, good-bye, or many other expressions in German depends on where you are in German-speaking Europe. What is appropriate in Berlin or Frankfurt may not sound right in Munich, Vienna (Austria), or Zurich (Switzerland). The following information will specify if a phrase is regional or not.

1

Much more than Americans, Germans shake hands when they meet and upon leaving (men and women alike). Be ready to shake hands (*der Handschlag*) when saying hello or good-bye.

Guten Morgen!   Good morning!
GOO-ten MOHR-ghen
Guten Abend!   Good evening!
GOO-ten AH-bent
Hallo!   Hello!
HAHL-lo

 Grüezi! *(GREW-tsee)*: Hello!

This is the standard greeting in German-speaking Switzerland (*die Schweiz*). Swiss German is difficult even for Austrians and Germans to understand, but all educated German Swiss can speak standard German (with a Swiss accent), and newspapers, books, and magazines are also published in standard German.

 Grüß Gott! *(grewce gott)*: Hello! (literally, "God's greeting!")

In Austria (*Österreich*) and the southern German state of Bavaria (*Bayern*), the standard greeting is different from that used in the rest of Germany. In these predominantly Catholic regions, a shortened form of "God greet you!" is the everyday way of saying hello. Among friends, family, and others whom you would address using *du* (the familiar "you" form), the common greeting is *Servus!* or *Grüß dich!* Like the Hawaiian "aloha," the German *Servus!* is also used to say "Farewell!" Another common Austrian/Bavarian farewell expression used strictly among friends and family is *Pfiat di!*

Servus!	Hello!
ZEHR-voos	
Grüß dich!	Hello!
grewce deekh	
Pfiat di!	Good-bye! (goes with *Grüß dich!*)
PFEE dee	

 Auf Wiedersehen! *(owf VEE-dare-zayn)*: Good-bye!

The standard German phrase for saying good-bye literally means "upon seeing you again." In daily use, this phrase is often shortened to *Wiedersehen!* It is used in the same context that you would use "Good-bye!" in English, but is also used when leaving a small shop or market, or even when leaving an apartment house elevator or a train compartment. Germans consider it impolite to simply leave without saying good-bye in such situations, even if it's the first time you've ever seen the people you are leaving.

 Tschüs! *(chewce)*: Bye!/Ciao!

Once reserved only for use among close friends, in recent years this form of good-bye (also spelled *tschüss*) has become as common as *Auf Wiedersehen!* in most of Germany (but not in Bavaria!). Similar to the Italian *ciao* (*tschau* in German), this northern German word of farewell (related to *adieu*) also has the variant *Tschüssi!*, which used to be strictly familiar but is now also heard in more formal situations where only *Auf Wiedersehen!* was once heard. In fact, in many parts of Germany, *Tschüs!* has largely replaced *Auf Wiedersehen!*

Note that in Austria and Bavaria, *Tschüs!* is usually frowned upon. There you should stick to the standard *Auf Wiedersehen!*, *Wieder-*

schauen! or, when appropriate, *Servus!* For these and other dialect or regional greetings, it is best to stick with the standard, more formal forms until you have a better understanding of how such phrases and expressions are used.

Tschüssi!	Bye!
chewce-see	

 Wie heißen Sie? *(vee HYCE-sen zee):* What's your name?

When a German-speaker asks you this question, the correct response is your last name, not your first. Another more formal way to ask this question is *Wie ist Ihr Name?*, but the answer is the same. German-speakers are not as quick to use first names as most English-speakers. Generally, the use of *Sie* (the formal "you") indicates a more formal, last-name situation. Don't be too quick to try to switch to *du* (the familiar "you") and first names. It can make some Germans uncomfortable, even if they go along with you in the switch. Wait for the German-speaker to suggest any change to a less formal relationship.

If you are talking to a child (under age 12 or so), you should ask *Wie heißt du?* The familiar *du* is reserved for children, pets, close friends, family and relations, and addressing God.

Wie ist Ihr Name?	What's your name?
vee ist ear NAH-muh	
Wie heißt du?	What's your name?
vee heist doo	

Ich heiße... *(eekh HYCE-suh):* My name is . . .

As with the question, a more formal answer is *Mein Name ist...*, using your last name.

Mein Name ist...   My name is . . .
myne NAH-muh ist

 Wie geht es Ihnen? *(vee gate es EE-nen):* How are you?

This is the standard (formal "you") German phrase used to ask how someone is. As in English, it will usually elicit a standard reply: *Gut, und Ihnen?* To ask a friend, a family member, or a child this question, you say *Wie geht's* (*dir*)?

Gut, und Ihnen?   Good, and you? (Fine, and you?)
goot oont EE-nen
Wie geht's (**dir**)?   How are you?
vee gates (deer)

 Das ist... *(dahs ist):* This is . . .

To introduce someone, you can use the simple phrase above. If you want to be a bit more formal, you can say *Darf ich...vorstellen?* Some examples:

Darf ich...vorstellen?   May I introduce . . . ?
darf eekh...FOR-shtel-len
Das ist meine Frau Linda.   This is my wife, Linda.
dahs ist MY-nuh frow LIN-da

Darf ich meine Frau Linda vorstellen? darf eekh MY-nuh frow LIN-da FOR-shtel-len	May I introduce my wife, Linda?
Das ist mein Mann Bob. dahs ist myne mahn bob	This is my husband, Bob.
Das ist mein Bruder Chuck. dahs ist myne BROO-dare chuck	This is my brother, Chuck.

 Das ist mein Freund Herr Schmidt. *(dahs ist myne froynt hair shmitt):* This is my friend, Herr (Mr.) Schmidt.

The German words *Freund* (male friend) and *Freundin* (female friend) are not used as casually as the English word "friend." The German word implies more than a casual friend or acquaintance (*Bekannter/ Bekannte*). The German word can also refer to a boyfriend or girlfriend, or even a significant other. Usually, *Freunde* are on *du*, first-name, terms, but when you introduce your friend to strangers, you would not use his/her first name in that situation.

 Das ist meine Freundin Frau Braun. *(dahs ist MY-nuh FROYN-din frow brown):* This is my (female) friend, Frau (Ms./Mrs.) Braun.

Any woman over the age of 18, married or not, is addressed as *Frau* (Ms./Mrs.). The use of *Fräulein* (Miss) is discouraged and used only for young ladies and girls. In the past, any waitress was addressed or called to the table with *Fräulein!* Today that is considered very bad manners, but the German language still has no good replacement term of address for getting the attention of a waitress (*Kellnerin*), other than waving politely and perhaps saying *Bitte!*

 Freut mich. *(froyt meekh)*: Pleased to meet you.

This standard phrase may be used during business and more formal introductions. The response is *Mich auch.*

Mich auch.	Me, too.
meekh owkh	

 Kennen Sie ihn/sie? *(KEN-nen zee een/zee)*: Do you know him/her?

German has two different verbs for "to know." The verb *wissen* is used for knowing a fact, whereas *kennen* is used for knowing a person or being familiar with something:

Wissen Sie, wo er ist?	Do you know where he is?
VIS-sen zee voh air ist	
Ja, ich kenne Hans, aber ich weiß nicht, wo er ist.	Yes, I know Hans, but I don't know where he is.
yah eekh KEN-nuh hahnz AH-bare eekh vice nikht voh air ist	

Danke! —Bitte! *(DAHNK-uh BIT-tuh):* Thanks!/Thank you! —You're welcome!

These two words are among the simple words and phrases that anyone traveling or living in a German-speaking country should know. Knowing such common expressions shows you have at least tried to learn some of the language. Being able to say "thank you" or "please" in German may seem like a small thing, but it will be appreciated.

Bitte is a very useful German word, not only because it's used for "you're welcome" but also because it's a polite way to ask people to do something: *Bitte* also means "please." This word can be thrown into just about any request to sound more polite, either as the first word or just about anywhere it fits: *Bitte, können Sie mir sagen...* or *Was kostet das, bitte?*

Danke is the shortest and easiest way to say "thank you" in German, but it's not always the best way. You also need to know that *danke* can mean "no, thank you" in certain situations! (More follows.)

Danke schön!	Thank you very much!
DAHNK-uh shern	
Danke sehr!	Thank you very much!
DAHNK-uh zehr	
Ich bedanke mich (sehr)!	I thank you (very much)!
eekh beh-DAHNK-uh meekh (zehr)	
Bitte, können Sie mir sagen...?	Please, can you tell me . . . ?
BIT-tuh KERN-nen zee meer ZAH-ghen	
Was kostet das, bitte?	What does that cost, please?
vahs KOST-et das BIT-tuh	

Nein, danke! *(nyne DAHNK-uh):* No, thanks!/No, thank you!

Saying "thank you" and "no, thank you" in German works pretty much the same way as in English, but if someone asks you if you would like something, and you reply with *Danke*, you won't get it. Because saying *Danke* in this situation is usually interpreted as *Nein, danke* (No, thanks.), you should say *Bitte* (Please.) or *Ja, bitte* if you want what is being offered.

Ja, bitte.   Yes, please.
yah BIT-tuh

 Danke schön! — Bitte schön! *(DAHNK-uh shern BIT-tuh shern):* Thank you very much! — You're welcome (very much)!

Notice the symmetry here! The German "thank you" phrase matches the "you're welcome" phrase in that both use *schön* ("very much," in this context). The same principle works for *Danke sehr!—Bitte sehr!* However, there are other ways to say "you're welcome," depending on the situation. For instance, if you have done someone a favor and he or she thanks you with *Vielen Dank!*, you could reply with *Gern geschehen!* or *Nichts zu danken!*

Danke sehr! — Bitte sehr!   Thank you very much! — You're
DAHNK-uh zehr BIT-tuh zehr   welcome (very much)!
Tausend Dank!   Many thanks! (literally "A thousand
TOW-zehnt dahnk   thanks!")

Vielen Dank!	Many thanks!/Thanks a lot!
FEEL-en dahnk	
Das ist sehr nett von Ihnen!	That is very nice/kind of you!
dahs ist zehr nett fonn EE-nen	
Gern geschehen!	Gladly done!/My pleasure!
ghern guh-SHAY-en	
Nichts zu danken!	Don't mention it!/It was nothing!
neex tsoo DAHNK-un	

 Nee. *(nay):* No./Nope.

If you really want to impress people with your German, learn the most common German word for "no"—even if it is rarely taught in German courses: *nee*. The use of this word in German is very similar to "nah" in English. It is easy to remember because it's pronounced like "nay," another way to say "no" in English. If you spend time around German-speakers, you'll hear *nee* much more often than *nein*. But *nein* also works fine.

 Doch! *(dohkh):* Yes! (in reply to a negative)

There is no real English equivalent for this common German word. It has at least a half dozen meanings, but it is often used to answer a negative question in the sense of "yes, on the contrary." An example: *Hast du keine Lust mit uns zu gehen?—Doch!* (Don't you feel like going with us?—Quite the contrary, yes!/Yes, I do feel like it!) The simple word *doch* makes it clear that you're contradicting the negative question. For a simple yes or no answer, just use *ja* or *nein*.

Ja.   Yes.
yah
Nein.   No.
nyne

 Jein. *(yine):* Yes and no. (Maybe.)

The slang word *jein* is a combination of *ja* and *nein* that means just that: "yes and no." Some more words of doubt are:

vielleicht   maybe, perhaps
fee-lykhte
ein bisschen   a little/a little bit
eyn BIS-shen

 Wie bitte? *(vee BIT-tuh):* Pardon? (I didn't catch that.)

This is the polite way to indicate that you didn't understand what someone said. Avoid the somewhat rude, less refined *Was?* This and the following phrases and expressions can help you deal with situations in which you need to have something repeated, said more slowly, or clarified.

Ich verstehe nicht.   I don't understand.
eekh fer-SHTAY-uh nikht
Langsamer, bitte.   Slower, please.
LONG-zahm-er BIT-tuh

Wiederholen Sie, bitte!	Please repeat that!
VEE-dare-hoh-len zee BIT-tuh	
Wie sagt man...?	How do you say...?
vee zahgt mahn	
Was?	What? Huh?
vahs	

 Das ist ausgezeichnet! *(dahs ist OWS-ge-tsyke-net):* That is fantastic/outstanding!

With this expression you can now state your approval (or disapproval) in German. Here are some more phrases you can use to express your opinion:

Das gefällt mir (nicht).	I (don't) like it.
dahs guh-FEHLT meer (nikht)	
Das ist ja toll!	That's great!
dahs ist ya tohl	

 Das ist der Hammer! *(dahs ist dare HAHM-mer):* That's great!

German *Hammer* phrases are usually positive and used to express strong approval, but they can also be used ironically or in a negative sense of surprise or reacting to something unexpected.

Das ist ein Hammer-Preis!	That's a great price!
dahs ist eyn HAHM-mer-pryce	

Sie sehen toll aus! *(zee ZAY-un tohl ows):* You look great! (formal)

If someone looks great, you may want to use this phrase (or the familiar form, shown in the following example sentence). Just be aware that Germans are often uncomfortable with such praise. But if you are expressing a genuine compliment, it should be fine.

Du siehst toll aus!	You look great! (familiar)
doo zeest tohl ows	
Das steht dir gut!	That looks good on you! (familiar)
dahs shtayt deer goot	
Das steht Ihnen gut!	That looks good on you! (formal)
dahs shtayt EE-nen goot	

 Es tut mir leid. *(ess toot meer lyte):* I'm sorry.

Normally, a simple "I'm sorry" will do, but if you are extremely sorry, you can add "really" (*wirklich*) or "very" (*sehr*) by saying: *Es tut mir wirklich/sehr leid.* To say "we are sorry," just change *mir* to *uns*: *Es tut uns leid.* You can't erase that mistake or faux pas, but you can apologize.

Es tut mir sehr/wirklich leid.	I'm very/really sorry.
ess toot meer zehr/VEERK-leekh lyte	
Es tut uns leid.	We're sorry.
ess toot oonz lyte	

Entschuldigung! *(ent-SHUL-dee-goong):* Excuse me!/Pardon me!

As in English, this word can also be used to introduce a polite question or request: *Entschuldigung, wo ist die Toilette?* or *Entschuldigung, können Sie mir helfen?* A slightly longer version is also very common, especially when you want to add "please": *Entschuldigen Sie, bitte....*

Entschuldigung, wo ist die Toilette? ent-SHUL-dee-goong voh ist dee toy-LET-tuh	Excuse me, where is the restroom?
Entschuldigung, können Sie mir helfen? ent-SHUL-dee-goong KERN-nen zee meer HEL-fen	Excuse me, can you help me?
Entschuldigen Sie, bitte... ent-SHUL-dee-ghen zee BIT-tuh	Excuse me, please . . .
Es war (nicht) meine Schuld. ess vahr (nikht) MY-nuh shult	It was (not) my fault.

 Leider können wir nicht kommen. *(LYE-der KERN-nen veer nikht KOHM-men):* Unfortunately we can't come.

Usually an introductory word, *leider* can also be placed within a sentence: *Er kann leider nicht kommen.* The phrase *Leider nicht* (LYE-der nikht) means *Unfortunately not/no* or *I'm afraid not.*

Er kann leider nicht kommen. Unfortunately, he can't come.
er kahn LYE-der nikht KOHM-men

Schade. Too bad./It's a shame.
SHAH-duh

Verzeihung! Excuse me!
fehr-TSEYE-oong

 Schönen Tag noch! *(SHER-nen tahk nokh):* Have a nice day!

A few more phrases in the same vein are:

Schönen Abend noch! Have a nice evening!
SHER-nen AH-bent nokh

Ein schönes Wochenende! Have a nice weekend!
eyne SHER-nes VOKH-en-en-duh

 Schon gut! *(shohn goot):* All right!/OK!

Besides the standard "OK" found in many languages, including German, you can say this phrase. To encourage someone to continue what he or she is doing, you can use these phrases:

Gut gemacht! Good job!/Good show!/Well done!
goot guh-MAHKT

Weiter so! Keep it up! (Keep doing what
VY-ter so you're doing!)

Halten Sie durch! Hang in there!/Hold on! (Don't give
HALL-ten zee durkh up the ship!) (formal)

Halt durch!
HALLT durkh

Hang in there!/Hold on! (Don't give up the ship!) (familiar)

(Mein) Kompliment!
myne komp-luh-MENT

My compliments!/Well done!

 Alles klar! *(ALL-es klahr):* Got it! (I understand what you've said!)

This phrase literally means "everything's clear," and falls into the category of everyday "formula" phrases commonly used but rarely found in phrase books. A few more are:

Genau!
guh-NOW

Exactly!/Right! (I couldn't agree more!)

Das hat mir gerade noch gefehlt!
dahs haht meer guh-RAH-duh
    nohkh guh-FAYLT

That's all I need (on top of everything else)!

Keine Ahnung.
KY-nuh AH-noong

I haven't a clue./I haven't the foggiest idea.

Mir reicht's!
meer rykhts

I've had it!/That's enough!

Chapter 2

Money Matters

 WIe viel Euro kostet das? *(vee feel OY-row KOST-tet dahs)*: How many euros does that cost?

Austria and Germany belong to the euro zone, those European Union (EU) countries in which the euro, or *der Euro* (dare OY-row), is the legal currency. Switzerland continues to use its Swiss franc (*Schweizer Franken*). The plural of *Euro* in German does not add an *s*: *zwei Euro* (two euros).

One euro has 100 euro cents, or *der Eurocent* (dare OY-row-tsent). In addition to the euro cent coins (in denominations of 1, 2, 5, 10, 20, and 50 cents), there are also one- and two-euro coins (*Münzen*).

Like the euro coins, euro notes vary in size (and color) for each denomination, ranging from the small five-euro note to the larger 500-euro note. Notes in normal circulation are in denominations of 5, 10, 20, 50, 100, 200, and 500 euros; however, the 100-euro and larger notes tend to be avoided in everyday commerce. (The 100-euro note is the most frequently counterfeited euro bill.)

Wie viel kostet das?	How much does that cost?
vee feel KOST-tet dahs	

 Gibt es eine Bank in der Nähe? *(gibt ess EYE-nuh bahnk in dare NAY-uh):* Is there a bank nearby?

There are three main kinds of banks in German-speaking Europe. A bank is called *eine Bank* (EYE-nuh bahnk), but there is also a public, not-for-profit savings and loan association (building society, in Britain) known as a *Sparkasse* (SHPAR-kahs-suh) or *Volksbank* (FOLKS-bahnk). The German post office (*Deutsche Post*) also offers banking services under its *Postbank* brand. For the average person they are all banks and function as banks. In any branch of these banks, you will find a *Geldautomat* (ATM, or cash machine) where you can obtain cash with your debit or credit card. You will also find ATMs in shopping centers, in larger stores, on the street in business districts, and in other public places. (See the ATM example sentences later in this chapter.)

Wo ist die Kasse?	Where is the cashier's window?
voh ist dee KAHS-suh	
Ich möchte Bargeld auf mein Konto einzahlen.	I'd like to deposit cash into my account.
eekh MERG-tuh BAR-gelt owf myn KOHN-toh EYN-tsah-len	
Ich möchte Bargeld von meinem Konto abheben.	I'd like to withdraw cash from my account.
eekh MERG-tuh BAR-gelt fonn MY-nem KOHN-toh AHB-hay-ben	

Wir haben keine Kasse. *(veer HAH-ben KY-nuh KAHS-suh):* We have no cash teller/cashier's window.

Since many German bank branches today have no cash teller window, this is a phrase you may hear, meaning that the only way to get cash or deposit cash is with an ATM in the bank. Look for a sign that says *Auszahlungen* (withdrawals) or *Einzahlungen* (deposits). Most machines allow you to withdraw cash with a credit or debit card (and display the Visa and MasterCard logos), but only those marked *Einzahlungen* can accept (and count) cash for deposit. Machines marked *Kontoauszüge* only provide a bank statement for account holders.

 Gibt es einen Geldautomaten in der Nähe? *(gibt ess EYE-nen GELT-ow-toh-MAH-ten in dare NAY-uh):* Is there an ATM nearby?

All ATMs, or cash machines (*Geldautomaten* in Germany, *Bankomaten* in Austria) in Europe offer a choice of languages (*Sprachen*), including English, usually indicated by flag icons. Simply choose English and then follow the instructions on the screen. The (usually green) Confirm or OK button is labeled *Bestättigen* or *Bestättigung* in German. A PIN code is called a *Geheimzahl: Bitte, geben Sie Ihre Geheimzahl ein.* (Please enter your PIN.)

Gibt es einen Bankomaten in der Nähe?

Is there an ATM nearby? (in Austria)

gibt ess EYE-nen BAHNK-oh-MAH-ten in dare NAY-uh

Gibt es eine Wechselstube in der Nähe? *(gibt ess EYE-nuh VEK-sel-SHTOO-buh in dare NAY-uh):* Is there a money exchange nearby?

In addition to banks, you can exchange money or cash traveler's checks at a *Geldwechsel* (GELT-vek-sel) or *Wechselstube* (VEK-sel-SHTOO-buh), or money exchange. These are found at airports, train stations, and other places frequented by travelers and tourists. You will be asked to present your passport, or *der Reisepass* (dare RYE-zuh-pahss), when cashing traveler's checks at either a bank or a money exchange.

 Wie ist der Wechselkurs heute? *(vee ist dare VEK-sel-koors HOY-tuh):* What's the exchange rate today?

Most banks and money exchanges have a sign with the current exchange rate (*der Wechselkurs*) posted near the entrance or in a window.

Ich möchte...wechseln.	I'd like to exchange . . .
eekh MERG-tuh...VEK-seln	
Ich möchte 500 Dollar wechseln.	I'd like to exchange $500.
eekh MERG-tuh fewnf HOON-dert DOL-lar VEK-seln	
Können Sie mir Zehner/Zwanziger geben?	Can you give me tens/twenties?
KERN-nen zee meer TSAY-ner/ TSVAN-tsig-er GAY-ben	
Ich hätte gern auch etwas Kleingeld.	I'd also like some change (coins).
eekh HET-tuh gehrn owkh ET-vahs KLINE-gelt	

Ich möchte Geld überweisen. *(eekh MERG-tuh gelt EW-ber-VYE-zen):* I'd like to transfer money/pay into an account.

A money transfer *(eine Überweisung* or *Geldüberweisung)* is the standard way to transfer money from person to person or from one account to another in German-speaking Europe. The German, Austrian, and Swiss banking systems do not use personal or business checks in the American or British sense. (There is no such thing as writing a personal check to pay for groceries or to pay a bill.) An *Überweisung* form can be filled out in writing or on a computer (online banking). In either case, you need the firm or person's name, account number, and bank code *(Bankleitzahl)* for each account. The forms are usually in both German and English.

 Nehmen Sie Kreditkarten? *(NAY-men zee kre-DIT-kar-ten):* Do you take credit cards?

German shopping rule number one: *Never* just assume that a shop or restaurant in the German-speaking countries will accept credit cards, or *Kreditkarten* (kre-DIT-kar-ten)! Unlike in the United States or even in neighboring France, credit card acceptance in Germany and Austria is mostly limited to the tourist circuit (hotels, rental car agencies, airline or rail tickets, etc.). Even some restaurants and shops in tourist areas may not accept credit cards. To avoid an unpleasant surprise, always ask before deciding to buy something or before you sit down in a restaurant.

Germans, Austrians, and the Swiss carry more cash, or *Bargeld* (bar-gelt), around than most Americans because cash payment is the norm for many situations in which it would be fairly rare in the United States or in other parts of Europe. Even some large bookstores, grocery, department, and electronic stores do not accept credit cards,

21

but they often have an ATM where you can use your debit or credit card to get cash for your purchase. Many stores and businesses that do not accept credit cards will accept EC (Maestro) card payment (a type of bank card), but you need a German or European bank account in order to get an EC card. Since it is easy to confuse the EC/Maestro bank card logo with the MasterCard logo, be aware that they are two different things.

 Nehmen Sie Reiseschecks? *(NAY-men zee RYE-zuh-shecks):* Do you take traveler's checks?

With ATMs and the popularity of online banking, the use of traveler's checks in Europe has declined in recent years. Today traveler's checks are usually just a backup for the electronic cash options. Other than the security they offer, another advantage of traveler's checks is that most banks and *Geldwechsel* offices pay a slightly better exchange rate for them than they do for cash. But many German shops and businesses do not like to accept or exchange traveler's checks. Even if they do, you generally get a poorer exchange rate than from a bank.

Kann ich diese Reiseschecks einlösen?	Can I cash these traveler's checks?
kahn eekh DEEZ-uh RYE-suh-shecks EYN-ler-zen	

Chapter 3

Accommodations

 Haben Sie ein Doppelzimmer? *(HAH-ben zee eyn DOP-pel-TSIM-mer):* Do you have a double (room)?

One of the first things a visitor to Germany will notice is the difference in bedding. The German *Federbett* (down filled comforter) replaces blankets and a top sheet. A so-called *Doppelbett* (double bed) is often two single beds next to each other (in one piece of furniture). Even a modest hotel (*das Hotel*) or B&B (*die Pension*) in Germany, Austria, or Switzerland will usually be clean, have an in-room bath, have a small in-room TV set, and offer a continental breakfast (*Frühstück*). Only more expensive hotels tend to offer king-size or queen beds. The typical German hotel room may seem a bit cramped by American standards. Despite the use of star ratings when talking about European hotels (*ein Vier-Sterne-Hotel* is a four-star hotel in German), the stars can mean different things in different countries. The hotel rating system is controlled by the hotel associations in each of the German-speaking countries, and there is no uniform EU rating system. (In Switzerland, a three-star hotel has a bath and TV in all rooms; in Germany even a one-star hotel must have that and a color TV with a remote.)

Fortunately, the quality of accommodations in Germany and the other German-speaking countries is generally quite good, and almost every hotel, even many smaller ones, can be found on the Web, making it easy to contact them and make reservations. Most hotel clerks speak English, but for those small, remote spots where you might need it, this section offers some key German phrases.

Ich möchte ein Einzelzimmer.	I'd like a single room.
eekh MERG-tuh eyn EYN-tsel- TSIM-mer	
Haben Sie ein Zimmer für drei Personen?	Do you have a room for three people?
HAH-ben zee eyn TSIM-mer fewr dry per-ZOHN-en	

 Ich möchte ein Zimmer mit Ausblick. *(eekh MERG-tuh eyn TSIM-mer mitt OWS-blick):* I'd like a room with a view.

In some locations in Germany, Austria, or Switzerland you may want a room that allows you to take in some of the scenery, but that can come with a price. Ask yourself how much time you will actually spend in your room during your stay. Maybe a quiet room is really what you want.

Ich möchte ein ruhiges Zimmer.	I'd like a quiet room.
eekh MERG-tuh eyn ROO-ig-es TSIM-mer	

Gibt es ein Badezimmer? *(gibt ess eyn BAH-duh-TSIM-mer)*: Is there a bathroom?

Not that many years ago, a room with a bathroom was not something you could take for granted in Europe, but times have changed. Today it is the norm, although you can still find inexpensive hotels that offer cheaper rooms with only a washbasin and without an en suite bathroom, meaning you have to go down the hall to a shared bathroom (*Bad*) or shower (*Dusche*). A common feature of European baths or showers is the so-called *Handdusche* (HANT-DOO-shuh), a handheld shower head, which is precisely what the name says. Remember also that Germans (and other Europeans) make a clear distinction between the toilet (*die Toilette, das WC*) and the bath (*das Bad*), which in older buildings may even be in separate rooms.

 Mit Frühstück? *(mitt FREW-shtewk)*: With breakfast?

Most of the time breakfast is included in the price of your room, but some hotels and pensions make breakfast optional at extra cost. Ask if you are not sure. The breakfast room is often labeled *Frühstückszimmer*. The typical German continental hotel breakfast consists of assorted bread rolls (*Brötchen* or *Semmeln*) with butter (*Butter*) and jam (*Marmelade* or *Konfitür*), cold cuts (*Aufschnitt*), cheese (*Käse*), fruit (*Obst*), and cereals (cornflakes, *Müsli*) with milk (*Milch*). Most of the time there will also be a cloth-covered basket filled with hot soft-boiled eggs (*Eier*), plus typical German eggcups (*Eierbecher*) and small spoons (*Eierlöffel*) for eating them. To drink, you'll have coffee/tea (*Kaffee/Tee*), orange juice (or the bottled stuff that passes for *Orangensaft* in Germany), and often apple juice (*Apfelsaft*) or other juices. If you would like coffee or tea, you can request:

Wir möchten Kaffee/Tee bitte.   We'd like coffee/tea please.
veer MERG-ten kah-FAY / TAY BIT-tuh

 Gibt es einen Aufzug? *(gibt ess EYE-nen OWF-tsookh):* Is there an elevator?

Even modest hotels in Germany usually have an elevator, but it may be only slightly larger than a telephone booth! While standard modern hotels always have an elevator of normal size, some older, smaller hotels with up to three floors may have no elevator at all. If climbing up the stairs with your luggage is a problem, ask the previous example question when making your reservation or when checking in.

 Ist das Zimmer klimatisiert? *(ist dahs TSIM-mer klee-MAH-tee-seert):* Is the room air-conditioned?

Most modern hotels in Europe today have air-conditioned rooms, but air-conditioning is still much less common in Germany than in the United States. Smaller hotels and pensions may have no air-conditioning or may have what seems like inadequate cooling to Americans. Most Germans consider air-conditioning a health hazard!

 Haben Sie Nichtraucherzimmer? *(HAH-ben zee nikht-ROW-kher-TSIM-mer):* Do you have nonsmoking rooms?

Unheard of only a few years ago, many German hotels today offer rooms for nonsmokers, and forbid smoking in the breakfast room and other public areas.

Haben Sie einen Computer für Gäste? *(HAH-ben zee EYE-nen kom-POO-tare fewr GHEST-uh):* Do you have a computer for guests?

If you don't have your own laptop with you, some hotels have a room or corner with one or two computers for guests. Usually there is a per-hour charge. If you do have your own computer, many modern hotels offer wireless or Ethernet in-room Internet access, almost always for a fee. Sometimes a nearby Internet café may be another option.

Gibt es W-Lan-Internetzugang im Zimmer?

Is there wireless Internet access in the room?

gibt ess vay-lahn-IN-ter-net-TSOO-gahng im TSIM-mer

 Gibt es eine Jugendherberge in der Nähe? *(gibt ess EYE-nuh YOO-ghent-hare-BARE-ghuh in dare NAY-uh):* Is there a youth hostel nearby?

For low-budget travelers there are several good options in Germany. The youth hostel (*Jugendherberge*) is a German invention (Richard Schirrmann's Altena castle hostel in 1912)! But in recent years the word *youth* has disappeared from *youth hostel*. The over 550 hostels in Germany now accept travelers of any age. No longer reserved just for students and their teachers, hostels now welcome entire families or individual travelers. The only condition is that you must be a member of a hostel association (www.hihostels.com). No longer the spartan places of yore, many German hostels are now in scenic and historic locations, and some even offer private rooms. During peak season or in popular locations, making a reservation is a good idea.

If you are into camping, Germany also has many campgrounds (*Campingplätze*), often also located in scenic areas.

For more comfort but still at budget prices, consider a private room (*Zimmer*) or a bed-and-breakfast (*die Pension* or *das Hotel garni*). Both offer a clean room with breakfast at a lower cost than most standard hotels.

 Wir brauchen mehr Handtücher/Badetücher. *(veer BROW-khen mare HANT-tew-kher/BAH-duh-TEW-kher):* We need more hand towels/bath towels.

Even modest hotels provide towels and linens, but on occasion you may need to provide your own soap, called *Seife* (ZYE-fuh), or shampoo, which looks and sounds the same in German: *Shampoo*.

Die Lampe (im Bad) funktioniert nicht. dee LAHM-puh (im baht) FOONK-shioh-neert nikht	The light/lamp (in the bathroom) is not working.
Der Fernseher ist kaputt. dare FEHRN-zay-er ist kah-PUT	The TV is broken/not working.
Die Toilette ist verstopft. dee TOY-let-tuh ist FEHR-shtopft	The toilet is clogged.
Es gibt kein heißes Wasser. ess gibt kyne HY-ses VAHS-ser	There is no hot water.

Chapter 4

Travel and Transportation

 Wo ist die Gepäckausgabe? *(voh ist dee guh-PECK-OWS-gah-buh):* Where is the baggage claim (area)?

Your first encounter with transportation in Germany is likely to be when your flight arrives at the airport, or *der Flughafen* (dare FLOOG-hah-fen). German airports have good international signage in both German and English with symbols that make it easy to find your way. Since most airline employees at European airports speak English, not much space here will be devoted to typical airline travel requests, but here are some basic helpful expressions, phrases, or words. Note: In Germany there is no charge for an airport luggage cart, or *der Gepäck-wagen* (dare guh-PECK-vah-ghen).

Ankunft—Abflug	Arrivals—Departures
Ausland—Inland	International—Domestic (flights)

Wo finde ich eine Toilette? *(voh FIN-duh eekh EYE-nuh toy-LET-tuh):* Where can I find a restroom?

Enjoy your last free public toilet in Germany! The airport is one of the few places in Germany where you don't have to pay to use the facilities. Even some bars and cafés charge customers for using the *WC* (vay-say), or restroom!

 Ihren Pass/Reisepass bitte. *(EAR-en pahss/RYE-zuh-pahss BIT-tuh):* Your passport, please.

International passengers in Europe are divided into two categories: EU citizens and non-EU citizens. Travelers carrying a U.S. or Canadian passport, or *der Reisepass* (dare RYE-zuh-pahss), should be in the non-EU line for passport control.

 Wie lange bleiben Sie in Deutschland? *(vee LAHNG-uh BLY-ben zee in DOYTSH-lahnt):* How long will you be staying in Germany?

The passport official may ask you how long you will be staying in Germany. American and Canadian citizens are allowed a visit of up to three months (90 days) without a visa.

Drei Wochen.	Three weeks.
dry VOKH-en	
Zwei Monate.	Two months.
tsvy MO-nah-tuh	
Vier Tage.	Four days.
feer TAH-guh	

Was ist der Grund Ihrer Reise?
vahs ist dare groont ear-er RYE-zuh

What is the purpose of your visit?

Ich bin geschäftlich hier.
eekh bin guh-SHEFT-likh here

I'm here on business.

Wir machen Urlaub.
veer MAHKH-en OOR-lowb

We're on vacation.

 Haben Sie etwas zu verzollen? *(HAH-ben zee ET-vahs tsoo fer-TSOL-en):* Do you have anything to declare?

After passport control and claiming your luggage, you'll pass though the customs (*Zoll*) area. Most travelers arriving in Germany will have no goods to declare and should follow the green line through the customs area. Sometimes there are spot checks and passengers are asked to open their bags, but normally you just walk through to the exit, or *Ausgang* (OWS-gahng).

Ich habe nichts zu verzollen.
eekh HAH-buh nikhts tsoo
    fer-TSOL-len

I have nothing to declare.

Ich möchte...verzollen.
eekh MERG-tuh...fer-TSOL-len

I would like to declare . . .

 Kommt der Flug planmässig an? *(kohmt dare floog PLAHN-may-sikh ahn):* Is the flight arriving on time?

For your connecting flight or other flights within Germany, you can use or may hear or read these phrases. The English word *gate* (*das Gate*), in its airport sense, has become more common than the German *der Flugsteig* in recent years.

Wann kommt der Flug an?	When does the flight arrive?
vahn kohmt dare floog ahn	
Fliegt der Flug planmässig ab?	Is the flight departing on time?
fleegt dare floog PLAHN-may-sikh ahp	
Wo ist mein Flugsteig? (mein Gate)	Where is my gate?
voh ist myne FLOOG-styge (myne gate)	
Der Flug hat zwanzig Minuten Verspätung.	The flight has a twenty-minute delay.
dare floog haht TSVAN-tsik mee-NOO-ten fer-SHPAY-toong	
Der Flug ist annulliert worden.	The flight has been canceled.
dare floog ist ahn-NOO-leert VOR-den	

 Wo bekomme ich ein Taxi? *(voh beh-KOHM-muh eekh eyn TAHX-ee):* Where can I get a taxi?

Before you take a taxi to your hotel or destination, consider a much cheaper alternative: public transportation (*öffentlicher Verkehr*). To get from the airport to the city, or to get around in the city, one good option is the excellent public transit system found in larger German cities. The Frankfurt and Munich airports each have their own train station (*Bahnhof*) with rail connections to downtown. The rail fare is much less than taking a taxi! (For rental-car phrases, see the Chapter 5.)

In most cases, your commuter rail ticket is also valid on all types of public transportation you may wish to use: bus, tram, metro (*U-Bahn*), or local rail (*S-Bahn*). Unlike in London, New York, or Paris, the rail and metro lines in Berlin, Cologne, Hamburg, Munich, and other large German cities have a flat-rate fare within set zones, and there are no entry and exit turnstiles at stations. A ticket is valid for up to two hours after validation on any local bus, train, or streetcar (but not on regional DB trains) for one-way travel to your destination. In most German cities, you can buy a ticket on a bus or streetcar but not on the underground (*U-Bahn*) or commuter trains (*S-Bahn*). (More below.)

Ist dieser Fahrschein gültig für Zonen A und B?	Is this ticket valid for zones A and B?
ist DEE-zer FAHR-shine gewl-tikh fewr TSOH-nen ah oont bay	
Wo kann ich umsteigen?	Where can I transfer?
voh kahn eekh OOM-shty-ghen	

 Wo kann ich eine Fahrkarte/einen Fahrschein kaufen?
(voh kahn eekh EYE-nuh FAHR-kart-uh/EYE-nen FAHR-shine KOW-fen): Where can I buy a ticket? (for the bus, tram, local train, etc.)

You usually purchase a ticket at a ticket machine (*Fahrkartenautomat*) that accepts coins, bills, and sometimes an EC (European) bank card (but usually not credit cards). The touch-screen machines offer a choice of languages, including English, but usually you will want *eine Einzelfahrkarte* (a single ticket) for the zone or zones you will be traveling in. In most cities you can also buy a *Sammelkarte* or *Streifenkarte*, which is a multi-ticket strip or booklet of four to six tickets at a reduced rate. There are also special all-day tickets (*Tageskarten*) and other special tickets aimed at tourists (*Touristenfahrkarten*). Larger stations have a ticket counter with a real person where you can also get a route map and a brochure (in German and English) about the fares and various tickets.

On the platform (*der Bahnsteig*) at S-Bahn or U-Bahn stations you will see red or yellow ticket validation machines (*der Entwerter* or *Entgelter*). You must insert your ticket to get it stamped before boarding the train. An unvalidated ticket is the same as no ticket! There are spot checks for ticket control, and if you are caught without a valid ticket there is a 40- to 60-euro fine, depending on the city. On a bus you can buy a ticket from the driver (in most cities) that is validated when you buy it. There is also a validation machine for tickets not bought on the bus. Trams usually have only automated ticket machines and validators.

Underground metro stations are indicated by a blue-and-white *U* sign for *U-Bahn*. Commuter rail stations have a green-and-white *S* for *S-Bahn*. Berlin, Hamburg, Munich, and other large German cities have excellent public transportation systems that make a car unnecessary, especially because it is so difficult to find a parking space.

Eine Übersichtskarte, bitte.	A route map, please.
EYE-nuh EW-ber-zeekhs-KAR-tuh BIT-tuh	
Welche Linie fährt nach...?	Which line for . . . ?
VELL-khuh LIN-ya fehrt nahkh	
Welche Richtung?	Which direction?
VELL-khuh REEKH-toong	

Notices you may see or hear:

Fahrscheine bitte vor Fahrtantritt entwerten.	Please validate your ticket before use.
Haltestelle	Bus stop, tram stop

Nächste Station(en)...	Next station(s) . . . (in S- or U-Bahn)
Nächster Halt...	Next stop . . . (in bus or tram)
Endhaltestelle.	Last stop. (end of the line)
Dieser Zug endet hier.	This train ends here. (end of the line)

 Zurückbleiben! *(tsoo-rewk-BLY-ben)*: Stand back!

This phrase is commonly heard in the S-Bahn and U-Bahn in Berlin when the train is about to depart. It may be heard in other variations in different cities with metros or commuter rail systems.

 Wo kann ich ICE-Fahrkarten kaufen? *(voh kahn eekh ee-say-ay-FAHR-kart-en KOW-fen)*: Where can I buy ICE (high-speed) train tickets?

You can buy train tickets, or *Bahnfahrkarten* (BAHN-fahr-kart-en), for regional or long-distance trips at a train station (*der Bahnhof*), travel bureau (*das Reisebüro*), or online. If you buy your ticket online (www .bahn.de, in German or English) with a credit card, you can print out an e-ticket with a bar code that the conductor will scan. But you must have the credit card you used to pay for the ticket with you on the train (as a security measure).

The privatized national German railway is commonly known as *die Bahn* (dee bahn), short for *Deutsche Bahn* (German Rail). The Deutsche Bahn, or DB (day-bay), has an extensive network of rail lines throughout Germany connecting travelers to almost any city or town of even moderate size. Ranging from regional (*Regio*) trains that stop frequently to high-speed Intercity Express (ICE) trains that cater to business travelers with hourly departures between major German cities, Germany's rail system is generally safe and reliable. Although it has its detractors (particularly regarding cost and customer service), Deutsche Bahn is definitely one of Europe's best rail operators.

Railroad stations have numbered tracks: *Gleis 4* (glyce feer), or Track 4. On the platform, or *Bahnsteig* (bahn-shtyge), you will usually see a *Wagenstandanzeiger* ("car indicator" sign) with a diagram of your train (each train has a number) showing where your numbered car/coach will be located when the train arrives. The letters A, B, C, D, etc. indicate where along the length of the platform your car will be standing. This makes it easier to find your car and avoid having to walk through the train to find your reserved seat.

 Erster oder zweiter Klasse? *(AIR-ster OH-dare TSVY-ter KLAHS-suh):* First or second class?

Whether you want to travel first or second class is one of the first decisions you must make before you buy a rail ticket. Each rail coach has a large number 1 or 2 by the door, indicating the class of the car. (Sometimes a single car will be split between first class on one end and second class on the other.) Besides the higher cost, the main difference is more room and comfort in first class. German long-distance trains usually offer two types of seating. The *Großraumwagen* is a standard "open space" car with rows of seats on each side and a center aisle. Compartment cars, or *Abteilwagen*, have a narrow hallway on one side with sliding doors to compartments that seat six people, three on each side.

Germany's passenger railway system also connects with many international destinations all across Europe. Austria and Switzerland also offer good rail connections. With the advent of low-fare airlines in Germany and Europe, rail is not always the cheapest or fastest option, but for distances under 300 miles (500 km), rail travel is difficult to beat.

If you want to buy your ticket at the station, here are some phrases to use:

Ich brauche eine Karte für eine einfache Fahrt nach... eekh BROW-kuh EYE-nuh KAR-tuh fewr EYE-nuh eyn-FAKH-uh fahrt nahkh	I need a one-way ticket to . . .
Ich brauche eine Rückfahrkarte nach... eekh BROW-kuh EYE-nuh REWK-fahr-kahr-tuh nahkh	I need a round-trip ticket to . . .
Muss ich umsteigen? MOOS eekh OOM shty ghen	Do I have to change trains?
Gibt es einen direkten Zug nach... gibt ess EYE-nen dee-REK-ten tsook nahkh	Is there a direct train to . . .

 Ich möchte auch eine Platzkarte. *(eekh MERG-tuh owkh EYE-nuh PLAHTS-kar-tuh):* I'd also like a seat reservation.

During peak travel periods, especially in the summer, it is a good idea to reserve a seat on your train for a slight extra fee. Reserved seats are indicated by a paper or electronic notice on the luggage rack above the seat row or in the aisle window of a compartment. The seat number is shown with the segment (between two cities) for which the reservation is valid. The person holding the *Platzkarte* has the right to that reserved seat.

Es gibt einen Zuschlag für den ICE. *(ess gibt EYE-nen TSOO-shlahg fewr dane ee-say-ay):* There is a surcharge for the ICE.

Unlike with air travel, you are much more likely to need German when traveling by rail in Germany. Although some ticket agents and conductors (once called *Schaffner*, but now known as *Zugbegleiter*, or train escorts) and other train personnel speak excellent English, many do not. A recent German bestseller lambasting DB was entitled: *senk ju vor träwelling* (the heavily German-accented pronunciation of "Thank you for traveling") with the sarcastic subtitle "How you can travel by rail and still arrive [at your destination]."

Chapter 5

Driving and the Autobahn

 Ich möchte ein Auto mieten. *(eekh MERG-tuh eyn OW-toe MEE-ten):* I'd like to rent a car.

All the major American and European car rental agencies, or *Autovermietung* (OW-toe-fer-MEE-toong), can be found in Germany, especially at the airport, major hotels, and other tourist locations. Counter personnel at most car rental agencies in Germany also speak English, so we will offer only a few key phrases just in case. There are two main words in German for *car* or *automobile*: *das Auto* (dahs OW-toe) and *der Wagen* (dare VAH-ghen), as in Volkswagen. They are pretty much interchangeable, and a rental car is either *ein Mietauto* (eyn meet-OW-toe) or *ein Mietwagen* (eyn meet-VAH-ghen).

 Ihren Führerschein, bitte. *(EAR-en FEWR-er-shine BIT-tuh):* Your driver's license, please.

This sentence is one you are bound to hear when renting a car. Your U.S. driver's license, or *Führerschein* (FEWR-er-shine), is valid for renting a car and driving in Germany (up to 90 days without a visa). Legally you are required to have a translation of your American license, although most people ignore this requirement, and it is possible to rent a car without an International Driving Permit (IDP), which is basically a translation of your state driver's license and can be obtained from AAA before your trip. Although the driving age in Germany is 18, most rental agencies require drivers to be at least 21 years old to rent a car.

 Haben Sie ein Auto mit Automatik? *(HAH-ben zee eyn OW-toe mitt OW-toe-MAH-tik):* Do you have a car with automatic transmission?

Most European rental cars have a manual (stick-shift) four- or five-speed transmission. You can rent a vehicle with automatic transmission, or *die Automatik* (dee OW-toe-MAH-tik), but it will cost more than a model with manual shift, or *das Schaltgetriebe* (shahlt-guh-TREE-buh). Although air-conditioned cars are more common in Europe than they used to be, you may want to ask to be sure.

Hat das Auto Klimaanlage?   Does the car have air-conditioning?
haht dahs OW-toe KLEE-muh-
   ahn-LAH-guh

 Kann ich ein Navi bekommen? *(kahn eekh eyn NAH-vee beh-KOHM-men):* Can I get a GPS navigator?

Although German highways are usually well marked, GPS navigation systems, or *Navis* (NAH-vees), short for *Navigationssystem*, are very popular in Europe and are offered as an option for rental cars. Just make sure the one you get offers English as a language option—or perhaps you *want* to learn more German by listening to your *Navi* giving you directions in German!

 Ist das ein Dieselwagen oder ein Benziner? *(ist dahs eyn DEE-zel-VAH-ghen OH-dare eyn ben-TSEEN-er):* Is that a diesel or a gas model?

Gasoline is called *Benzin* (ben-TSEEN) in German, but to "step on the gas" is *gas geben* (gas GAY-ben). The diesel engine, or *der Dieselmotor* (dare DEE-zel-mo-TOR) is named for its German inventor, Rudolf Diesel (1858–1913). Diesel-powered cars have long been popular in Germany, but the days of cheaper diesel fuel may be over. Today the only advantage of modern diesel engines is better fuel consumption compared to gasoline engines. Diesel fuel for passenger cars is widely available in Europe. All gasoline sold in Germany today is *bleifrei* (unleaded, or lead free).

Be prepared for fuel price shock! The average price of diesel fuel or gasoline in Germany is usually about twice the U.S. average. A major portion of the price per liter goes to taxes to help pay for roads and Germany's free autobahns.

Ich hätte lieber einen Diesel/ Benziner.	I'd prefer a diesel/gasoline model.
eekh HET-tuh LEE-ber EYE-nen DEE-zel/ben-TSEEN-er	

Haben Sie etwas größer/kleiner? *(HAH-ben zee ET-vahs GREW-ser/KLYNE-er):* Do you have something larger/smaller?

Although European cars tend to be on the small side, you may need something a bit larger if you have luggage and several people traveling together. Larger vehicles, SUVs, and vans are available if you need them. But if a smaller car will do, you'll save on both fuel costs and rental fees.

 Was ist die Geschwindigkeitsgrenze? *(vahs ist dee guh-SHVIN-dig-kytes-GRENTS-uh):* What is the speed limit?

Germany's network of autobahns is legendary. Technically and legally, there is no overall official speed limit for cars on the German autobahn, but finding a stretch of it today without any posted speed limit is increasingly difficult. You are much more likely to find a *Stau* (shtow), or traffic jam, and many autobahn segments have a posted speed limit, or *Geschwindigkeitsbegrenzung* (guh-SHVIN-dig-kytes-beh-GRENTS-oong), of 120 km/h (75 mph) or less, especially in urban areas. The Austrian and Swiss autobahns do have a legal speed limit of 130 km/h (81 mph), which is also the "suggested" German limit.

The speed limit on German two-lane highways is always 100 km/h (62 mph), whether posted or not. In towns it is always 50 km/h (31 mph), unless posted otherwise. This begins as soon as you pass the yellow town-limit sign. Most German towns and cities also have so-called *30-Zonen* (30 km/h, 19-mph zones) in residential areas to reduce noise and to make it safer for children. Speed limit signs with a *bei Nässe* (when wet) sign beneath them indicate the limit for wet conditions.

Wo wird's geblitzt? *(voh veerts guh-BLITST):* Where are the radar speed traps?

The speed limit on German roads and highways is enforced by both stationary and mobile radar/photo devices that take a picture of the driver and the license plate. Usually you won't know you got a speeding ticket until it arrives in the mail (forwarded by the rental car company). German radio stations report the speed traps of the day in and around larger cities.

 Wo kann ich eine Autobahn-Vignette kaufen? *(voh kahn eekh EYE-nuh OW-toe-vin-YET-tuh KOW-fen):* Where can I buy an autobahn sticker?

Germany has an autobahn toll, or *Maut* (mowt), for trucks but not for cars. In Austria and Switzerland your car must have a special sticker, or *eine Vignette* (EYE-nuh vin-YET-tuh), affixed to the windshield in order to drive on the autobahn there. If you're lucky, your rental car will already have *eine Vignette*. If not, you'll have to buy one at the border or at a gas station before getting on an autobahn. Switzerland has a flat rate for all drivers, but the Austrian autobahn stickers are available for various time periods, from ten days to a year. Motorcycles are also subject to the autobahn vignette toll. Trucks pay a per-kilometer fee. There is a stiff fine for driving on the autobahn without a sticker in Austria and Switzerland. Austria and Switzerland also have a few private turnpikes and tunnels, usually in mountainous regions, for which you need to pay an extra toll not covered by the sticker.

The most important thing to watch for when driving on the autobahn is faster vehicles passing you, and seemingly coming out of nowhere, since they are often moving at speeds exceeding 145 km/h (90 mph). This high speed makes it easy to understand why it is illegal to pass other vehicles on the right on the autobahn or any multilane roadway in Germany (unless traffic is moving at a very slow speed in both lanes—under 60 km/h [35 mph]—and then only at a speed no higher than 15 mph faster than the traffic in the left lane).

 Wie hoch ist die Geldstrafe? *(vee hohkh ist dee GELT-shtrahf-uh):* How much is the fine?

Now that you have your rental car, do you know the driving laws in Germany and Europe? Some of them are different from those in the United States, and you could run into problems if you're not aware of the differences. Being a foreigner does not excuse you from following the law or from paying a fine if you don't.

The most important rule of the road in Europe that you must know concerns right-of-way, or *Vorfahrt* (FOR-fahrt). Vehicles coming from the right at an intersection always have the right-of-way. Unless there is a sign or traffic signal indicating otherwise, you must always yield to vehicles coming from the right. Because of this rule, Germany has far fewer stop and yield signs than is typical in the United States.

You should also recognize the European right-of-way sign: a yellow diamond on a white background. If you are driving on a road marked by this *Vorfahrtszeichen*, you have the right-of-way and vehicles coming from intersecting roads must yield to traffic on the main road.

 Wie komme ich nach...? *(vee KOHM-muh eekh nahkh):* How do I get to . . . ?

Traffic signs in Europe are standardized and use symbols that largely make words unnecessary. (A rare exception is *STOP*, used for stop signs throughout Europe.) You should become familiar with the various signs that tell you the speed limit, when you can pass, where you can park, etc. Directional and highway signs never say East, North, South, or West, even on the autobahn. They always simply indicate the next large (or small) town, so you must know which cities and towns are found along your route. Logically, autobahn numbers begin with an *A* (A2, A8, etc.) and regular highways (*Bundesstraßen*) with a *B* (B32, B55, etc.). To get on an autobahn you follow the blue town or city signs and the blue entrance sign that says *Einfahrt* (autobahn entrance). In Switzerland the autobahn signs are green.

 Wie weit ist es zur nächsten Raststätte? *(vee vite ist ess tsoor NEX-sten RAHST-shtet-tuh):* How far is it to the next rest stop/ service area?

Along most stretches of the German autobahn network and European turnpikes/freeways you will find *Raststätten*, where you can fill the tank, dine, visit the restroom (*WC*), and more. A service area is called a *Rasthof* if it also has a motel. The more modest *Rastplatz* (RAHST-plahts) usually has only restrooms and picnic tables.

 Ausfahrt *(OWS-fahrt):* Exit (on the autobahn)

Look for this sign when it is time to leave the autobahn. You will see large blue signs showing the cities or towns accessed via the next exit. There are also signs that indicate the distance to the *Ausfahrt* (500 m, 200 m).

Wie komme ich nach Berlin?   How do I get to Berlin?
vee KOHM-muh eekh nahkh
    bare-LEEN

**Wie komme ich zum Stadtzen-   How do I get to the town center?
trum?**
vee KOHM-muh eekh tsoom
   SHTAHT-tsen-troom

 Wie heißt diese Straße? *(vee hyst DEES-uh SHTRAHS-suh):*
What's the name of this street?

Navigating within German cities can be tricky. As in most of Europe, the name of a German street (*die Straße, der Weg*), avenue (*die Allee*), lane (*die Gasse*), or boulevard (*der Boulevard*) often changes from one block to the next. Street signs may be on the corner of a building instead of on a pole. Having a good city map, *der Stadtplan* (dare SHTAHT-plahn), or GPS (see *Navi*, discussed previously) is essential when trying to find an apartment building, house, or business address in even medium-size towns.

In an effort to eliminate intersections, stop signs, and traffic signals—and avoid having many cars standing still with their engines running—Germany has an increasing number of traffic circles or roundabouts (*Kreisverkehr*), although they are much more common in France. The key to negotiating a German traffic circle is to remember that traffic already within the circle has the right-of-way. You should signal before turning out of the circle (but not when entering it!). Some large traffic circles in big cities have traffic lights you must follow, but normally you just go with the flow, keeping an eye out for the sign indicating the street or destination you want. Stopping your vehicle in a traffic circle is never a good idea! (It is also against the law.) If you miss your turn, simply go around one more time and exit.

Radweg *(RAHT-vayk):* Bike lane/path

Almost any German town or city of any size has marked bike lanes along many streets. But it is in big cities like Berlin, Frankfurt, or Munich (with heavy bike and auto traffic) where you must be especially careful to watch for cyclists coming from behind you when making a right turn. Cyclists have the right-of-way!

Even as a pedestrian you must be cautious about bike lanes. Should you happen to accidentally venture into a bike path while walking along a sidewalk, you could get run down by someone zooming along on a bicycle. Bike lanes are marked by white stripes and bike symbols on the sidewalk (or street). Round blue signs also designate bike lanes and sidewalks that are dual use (bikes and pedestrians side by side).

 Gibt es eine Tankstelle in der Nähe? *(gibt ess EYE-nuh TAHNK-shtel-luh in dare NAY-uh):* Is there a gas station nearby?

Virtually all gas stations in Germany today are self-serve *(Selbstbedienung)*. This is also one of the few instances in German-speaking Europe where a credit card is essential. Almost always you insert your card at the pump (much like an ATM) and get your credit card receipt *(Beleg)* after filling up *(volltanken)*. If you insist on paying cash, you usually must go inside to the cashier and pay in advance. (You'll also need to know your basic numbers in German in order to tell the cashier your pump number: *eins, zwei, drei...*) Most of the time, a single pump will have a choice of diesel and various grades of unleaded fuel.

If you need air *(Luft)* in your tires, there is usually a place for that off to the side, but it may cost you a few coins. (Nothing is free in Germany.) If you need service beyond that, you may want to find a station with an attendant, but those are rare these days.

Most *Tankstellen* in Germany are also mini-marts where you can buy snacks and some groceries; a road map, or *eine Straßenkarte* (EYE-nuh SHTRAH-sen-kar-tuh); coffee; soft drinks; and so on. They are also very popular with non-motorists on Sunday, when everything else in Germany is closed.

 Wo ist der Parkscheinautomat? *(voh ist dare PARK-shine-OW-toh-maht):* Where is the parking permit machine?

Finding a parking space in most German cities can be a very frustrating experience. If you are lucky enough to find one, most of the time you'll have to pay for it. Free on-street parking is very rare in Europe. If you don't see parking meters (*Parkuhren*), look for parking signs and the *Parkscheinautomat,* with a sign reading *Hier Parkschein lösen.* (Obtain your parking permit here.) Parking meters and parking discs (to indicate the time you parked) are becoming rare, now increasingly replaced by a type of vending machine that produces a *Parkschein* (parking permit/ticket) in exchange for your euro coins or, in some cases, a cell phone text message or a credit card/EC card payment. You place the *Parkschein* on your dashboard, and it specifies the time you have paid for. If you fail to buy a ticket or it expires before you return, you may find a *Knöllchen* (slang for a parking fine) on your windshield when you return to your car.

 Gibt es ein Parkhaus in der Nähe? *(gibt ess eyn PARK-house in dare NAY-uh):* Is there a parking garage (car park) nearby?

Public parking garages are another good option. Look for a blue sign with a white *P* for *Parkhaus.* Often located underground, and thus called *eine Tiefgarage* (EYE-nuh TEEF-guh-RAH-juh), "a deep garage," you will find these parking garages underneath public squares, or in shopping centers if above ground, in which case they are called *ein Parkhaus* (eyn PARK-house). Usually there is an electronic sign near the entrance that indicates how many parking spaces are still available, or *frei* (fry). Take the ticket you received at the entry gate (and keep it with you, not in the car), and be sure to note on which level (*Ebene*) and in which zone (often color-coded) you have parked. Some German parking garages use electronically coded round plastic tokens instead of paper tickets, but the procedure for paying is the same. (See the following information.)

Gibt es eine Tiefgarage in der
  Nähe?
gibt ess EYE-nuh TEEF-guh-RAH-juh
  in dare NAY-uh

Is there an underground parking
  garage nearby?

 Wo ist der Kassenautomat? *(voh ist dare KAHS-sen-OW-toh-maht):* Where is the cashier machine?

You must pay at the *Kassenautomat* located inside the garage before you go to your car, because you need your paid ticket to open the tollgate and exit the garage. Insert the ticket (or token) you received when you entered, and the *Kassenautomat* determines how much you owe (cash or credit-card payment) and encodes your exit ticket. Go to your car and follow the *Ausfahrt* (Exit) signs, insert your paid ticket to open the gate, and you're done. No humans involved, other than you!

Chapter 6

Shopping

Wie komme ich zum Marktplatz? *(vee KOHM-muh eekh tsoom MARKT-plahts):* How do I get to the market square?

Besides the traditional market square, often next to the town's largest cathedral or church, you will also find modern shopping centers *(das Einkaufszentrum)* and pleasant pedestrians-only shopping streets *(Fußgängerzone)* in even moderate-size cities, with boutiques and shops of all kinds.

Ich suche ein Kaufhaus. *(eekh ZOO-khuh eyn KOWF-house):* I'm looking for a department store.

Continental Europe's largest department store is Berlin's Kaufhaus des Westens, better known as *KaDeWe* (kah-day-vay). But Berlin is also home to a branch of the French department-store chain Galeries Lafayette and other German department stores, including Galeria Kaufhof and Karstadt. All large cities in German-speaking Europe have several department stores. The German-owned Woolworth stores offer bargain shopping. The C&A (say oont ah) chain is a popular chain of clothing stores.

Traditionally, German department stores had only two major sales per year, the *Sommer-* and the *Winterschlußverkauf* (end-of-summer and end-of-winter sale), but today sales are more frequent. Look for these signs: *Ausverkauf* (Sale), *Reduziert* (Reduced), *Rabatt* (Discount), *Sonderangebot* (Special), and even *Sale* in English.

All German department stores have a directory, often in both German and English, that tells you where you can find various items or departments (*Abteilungen*). It is usually found near the elevator (*der Aufzug*) or the escalator (*die Rolltreppe*). Keep in mind that floors are numbered differently in Europe; so, for example, the third floor in the United States is the second floor in Germany. The ground floor is labeled "E" (for *Erdgeschoss*) or "P" (for *Parterre*), both meaning the "ground floor," and sometimes just plain "0" (zero). The first floor above the ground is the first floor (*erste Etage, erster Stock*) in Europe.

Wo finde ich Handtaschen?	Where can I find purses?
voh FIN-duh eekh HAHNT-tahsh-en	
Handtaschen finden Sie in der	You'll find purses on the second floor.
zweiten Etage.	(third floor in the U.S.)
HAHNT-tahsh-en FIN-den zee in dare	
TSVY-ten eh-TAH-juh	

 Wann haben Sie geöffnet? *(vahn HAH-ben zee guh-ERF-net)*: What time do you open?

German, Austrian, and Swiss shopping hours (*Ladenöffnungszeiten*) are among the most restrictive in Europe. But it used to be even worse. Not that long ago most stores in German-speaking Europe closed at 6:00 P.M. on weekdays and even earlier on Saturday. That has changed for the better in recent years, but Sunday remains a no-shopping day. (Except for *verkaufsoffene Sonntage,* "shopping Sundays," when large stores and shopping centers are open from 1:00–8:00 P.M., for a maximum of ten times per year, depending on the state you're in.) With the exception of restaurants and tourism-related businesses, you must go to a gas station (*Tankstelle*) mini-mart, train station (*Bahnhof*), or airport (*Flughafen*) to buy anything on Sunday in Germany and Austria.

Although it is now legal for shops and businesses to open when they choose on Monday through Saturday, only larger stores actually stay open later than 8:00 P.M. Most smaller businesses are still open only from 9:00 A.M. to 6:00 P.M. Some department and grocery stores remain open until 10:00 P.M., a few even until midnight. Bakeries, called *die Bäckerei* (dee BECK-er-eye), open very early and may even be open on Sunday, especially if they also have a café.

 Wie viel kostet das? *(vee feel KOST-et dahs):* How much is that?

In most of Europe, including the German-speaking countries, the price of an item or service includes the sales tax or value-added tax, the VAT (*Mehrwertsteuer*). In other words, the price on the tag is what you will pay, including tax. Your cash register receipt will indicate the amount of tax you paid (usually 19 percent in Germany, 20 percent in Austria).

Das ist zu teuer.   That is too expensive.

dahs ist tsoo TOY-er

Haben Sie etwas billiger?   Do you have something cheaper?

HAH-ben zee ET-vahs BIL-lig-er

 Kann ich dies anprobieren, bitte? *(kahn eekh dees AHN-pro-BEER-en BIT-tuh)*: Can I try this on, please?

Clothing sizes in Germany are usually metric, but you will also see S, M, L sizes. Labels are sometimes also in English and often have icons for washing and care instructions.

Wo sind die Umkleidekabinen?   Where are the fitting rooms?

voh zint dee OOM-klye-duh-kah-
    BEAN-en

Es passt (mir) nicht.   It doesn't fit (me).

es pahsst meer nikht

Haben Sie etwas größeres/   Do you have anything larger/smaller?

    kleineres?

HAH-ben zee ET-vahs GREW-ser-es/
    KLYNE-er-es

Ich nehme das.   I'll take that one.

eekh NAY-muh dahs

 Nehmen Sie Kreditkarten? *(NAY-men zee kreh-DITT-kar-ten)*: Do you take credit cards?

Cash or credit? Shopping in the German-speaking countries, except for the different language, is pretty much like shopping in English. But there are a few things you need to know. One of the most important is the fact that Germany, Austria, and Switzerland are not nearly as credit-card friendly as are the United States and most other countries. Though hotels and most travel or tourist-oriented enterprises accept credit cards, you should not assume that all restaurants and shops will. Even the German railway, *Deutsche Bahn*, did not begin accepting credit cards until 1992!

Many stores—including bookstores, department stores, and supermarkets—and most restaurants off the tourist circuit do not accept credit cards. German-speaking Europe is a cash economy in many ways. It is wise to ask about this before making a purchase or sitting down in a restaurant. If the reply is *nein* (nyne), or "no," to your credit card question, you'll need to pay in cash. Even some smaller hotels (*Pension* or *Hotel-Pension*) and B&Bs (*Pension*, *Zimmer*) do not accept credit cards. If you need to get cash, you can go to a nearby ATM (*Geldautomat*) or bank and use your debit or credit card to obtain euros or Swiss francs. (See Chapter 2, "Money Matters," for more on these topics.)

The bottom line: Always carry enough cash, just in case. If you are able to use a credit card, you may hear:

Bitte unterschreiben Sie hier.   Please, sign here.
BIT-tuh oon-ter-SHRY-ben zee here

 Wo finde ich eine Drogerie? *(voh FIN-duh eekh EYE-nuh DRO-guh-ree):* Where can I find a drugstore?

If you need toiletries, beauty products, cosmetics, or household products in Germany, you can buy them at a *Drogerie* (and in department stores and supermarkets), not at an *Apotheke* (pharmacy). (See Chapter 13, "Health Issues," for more on this topic.) The three largest German drugstore chains are dm, Rossmann, and Schlecker. The German versions of the drugstore (*Drogerie/Discountmarkt*) also sell snack food, wine, paper products, photo supplies, and herbal medicines and teas.

 Öffnungszeiten *(ERF-noongs-TSY-ten):* Opening hours, business hours

Store hours are indicated in twenty-four-hour time: 22.00 is 10:00 P.M., for example. Here are some more common German terms seen in businesses, shops, and markets: *geöffnet/offen* (open), *geschlossen* (closed), *durchgehend geöffnet* (open all day, no lunch break), *über Mittag geschlossen* (closed for lunch), *montags Ruhetag* (closed Mondays; regular day off for smaller restaurants).

Some signs you may see while shopping: *Ausgang* (exit, way out), *Eingang* (entrance), *Kasse/Kassa* (cashier), *Umkleidekabine* (dressing room, fitting room).

 Darf ich Ihnen helfen? *(darf eekh EE-nen HELF-en):* May I help you?

Although German customer service often gets a bad rap in the land where the customer is not always king, you may be pleasantly surprised by the knowledgeable help you can get in the traditional *Fachgeschäft*, a shop that specializes in a particular product or service. Such businesses include: *Blumenladen* (florist), *Buchhandlung* (bookstore), *Bürobedarf* (office supplies), *Fotogeschäft* (photo store), *Optiker* (optician), *Schreibwarengeschäft* (stationery store), and *Spielwarengeschäft* (toy store).

Was darf es sein?	What would you like?
vahs darf ess zyne	
Was möchten Sie?	What would you like?
vahs MERG-ten zee	
Sonst noch etwas?	Will there be anything else?
sonst nohkh ET-vahs	

 Ich sehe mich nur herum. *(eekh SEH-uh meekh noor hair-OOM):* I'm just looking.

Most of the time, German salespeople will leave you alone. If you want help, you can get a clerk's attention with a friendly *Bitte* (BIT-tuh), or "Please."

Haben Sie...?	Do you have . . . ?
HAH-ben zee	
Das gefällt mir.	I like that (one).
dahs guh-FELLT meer	
Das ist alles.	That's all/everything.
dahs ist ALL-us	

 Wo ist die Kasse, bitte? *(voh ist dee KAH-suh BIT-tuh):* Where is the cashier/checkout stand, please?

At the checkout stand you can usually read the amount you owe on the cash register/computer display.

Das macht 34.95 Euro.	That comes to 34.95 (34 euros and
dahs mahkht feer-oont-DRY-sikh	95 cents).
OY-row FEWNF-oont-NOYN-zikh	

Chapter 7

Laundry and Good Grooming

Gibt es einen Waschsalon in der Nähe? *(gibt ess EYE-nen VAHSH-sah-lohn in dare NAY-uh):* Is there a Laundromat nearby?

Sooner or later just about every traveler needs a Laundromat or dry cleaner. Although hotels often offer cleaning services, it can be very pricey. Fortunately, it is fairly easy to find a *Waschsalon* in any medium- to large-size city in German-speaking Europe. If asking someone if there is a Laundromat nearby does not get you a good answer, try the Yellow Pages (*Gelbe Seiten*) or do a Web search for *Waschsalon* and the city you're in.

Most Laundromats have a large sign listing the prices for washing, drying, and detergent. Some use a computerized control panel where you select your machine and the washing cycle you want before paying (euro coins and bills, but usually not credit cards). There is rarely an attendant working there, of whom you can ask questions, so it helps to know the following German Laundromat vocabulary:

Waschen, das Waschen   to wash, washing
VAHSH-en

Waschmaschine   washer, washing machine
vahsh-ma-SHEEN-uh
Waschpulver   detergent
vahsh-PULL-fair
trocknen, das Trocknen to dry, drying
TROHK-nen

 Ich möchte diese Wäsche waschen lassen. *(eekh MERG-tuh dee-zuh VESH-uh VAHSH-en LAHS-sen):* I'd like to have these things washed.

A few full-service *Waschsalons* also offer to do the washing and drying for you, for an extra fee, of course. You can leave your wash there and pick it up later.

 Ich möchte diesen Anzug/dieses Kleid reinigen lassen.
(eekh MERG-tuh DEEZ-en AHN-tsook/DEEZ-es klite RINE-ee-ghen LAHS-sen): I'd like to get this suit/this dress dry cleaned.

Dry cleaning, or *chemische Reinigung* (KHEM-ish-uh RINE-ee-goong), is not cheap in Germany, but sometimes it is the only way to get the cleaning you need. Additional dry-cleaning concerns might be:

Können Sie das aufbügeln?   Can you press this?
KERN-nen zee dahs OWF-bew-geln
Können Sie diesen Fleck   Can you get this stain out?
   entfernen?
KERN-nen zee DEE-zen fleck
   ent-FAIR-nen

Können Sie das reparieren? *(KERN-nen zee dahs rep-ah-REER-en):* Can you repair this?

I hope you won't need to get something fixed during your time in Germany, but if your watch, camera, car, laptop, or something else goes on the fritz, here are some phrases to use to get repairs and services in specialty shops and department stores in Germany and other countries:

Können Sie es/sie reparieren, während ich warte?
Can you repair it/them while I wait?

KERN-nen zee ess/zee rep-ah-REER-en
VER-ent eekh VAHR-tuh

Wie viel wird die Reparatur kosten?
How much will the repair cost?

vee feel veert dee rep-ah-rah-TOOR
KOST-en

Wann kann ich es/sie abholen?
When can I pick it/them up?

vahn kahn eekh ess/zee AHP-hoh-len

 Gibt es einen Schuhmacher in der Nähe? *(gibt ess EYE-nen SHOO-makh-er in dare NAY-uh):* Is there a shoemaker nearby?

In larger cities it is still common to see shoemakers and shoe repair shops *(Schuhreparatur)*. Thrifty Germans like to get a lot of mileage out of their shoes and boots.

Ich möchte diese Schuhe/Stiefel reparieren lassen. eekh MERG-tuh DEEZ-uh SHOO-uh/ SHTEE-fel rep-ah-REER-en LAHS-sen	I'd like to get these shoes/boots repaired.
Dieser Absatz ist kaputt. DEEZ-er AHB-sahts ist kah-PUT	This heel is broken.
Die Sohle ist durchgelaufen. dee SOH-luh ist DURKH-guh-low-fen	The sole is worn down.

 Können Sie das ändern? *(KERN-nen zee dahs EN-dern):* Can you alter this?

For clothing alterations, look for a *Schneider* or *Schneiderei* (tailor), or more specifically an *Änderungsschneider(ei)*. In larger cities they are easy to find.

Das ist zu lang/zu kurz. dahs ist tsoo long/tsoo koorts	This is too long/too short.
Wann wird es fertig sein? vahn veert ess FAIR-tik zyne	When will it be ready?

 Ich suche einen Friseur. *(eekh ZOO-khuh EYE-nen free-zewr):* I'm looking for a barber/a hairdresser.

German hair salons (*Friseursalons*) are generally unisex shops, serving both women and men. In contrast with the traditional U.S. barber shop, most German barbers are women: *die Friseurin* (FREE-zewr-in). Some shops are either a *Damenfriseur* (women's hair salon) or a *Her-*

renfriseur (men's barber), but this is less common. For both men and women, getting your hair done means getting a shampoo along with your styling/cut. If you don't want a shampoo, request: *Ohne Waschen bitte* (OH-nuh VAHSH-en BIT-tuh).

Most hair salons take reservations, but you can usually walk in and get your hair cut or styled after a short wait. What kind of *Frisur* (free-ZOOR), or hairstyle, do you want?

Ich möchte einen Termin für heute/morgen.	I'd like an appointment for today/tomorrow.
eekh MERG-tuh EYE-nen tare-MEEN fewr HOY-tuh/MORG-en	
Ich möchte einen Haarschnitt.	I'd like a haircut.
eekh MERG-tuh EYE-nen HAHR-shnitt	
Schneiden und fönen, bitte.	A cut and blow-dry, please.
SHNYE-den oont FERN-en BIT-tuh	
Ich möchte eine Dauerwelle.	I'd like a perm.
eekh MERG-tuh EYE-nuh DOW-er-VELL-uh	
Eine Färbung, bitte.	Dye my hair, please.
EYE-nuh FAIR-boong BIT-tuh	
Eine Tönung, bitte.	A color rinse, please.
EYE-nuh TERN-oong BIT-tuh	
Bitte nicht zu kurz.	Not too short, please.
BIT-tuh nikht tsoo koorts	
Bitte ein bisschen kürzer.	A little shorter, please.
BIT-tuh EYN BIS-shen KEWRTS-er	

Chapter 8

Food and Drink

 Möchten Sie etwas bei der Café-Konditorei haben?
(MERG-ten zee ET-vahs by dare kah-FAY-kon-DIT-oh-RYE HAH-ben):
Would you like to have something at the Café-Konditorei?

A *Café-Konditorei* serves coffee and pastries in many varieties. It is a good place to relax and enjoy a refreshing *Café macchiato* (latte macchiato) with some *Apfelstrudel* (AHP-fel-SHTROO-del), or apple strudel, or other similar drinks and pastries. You will also find many Starbucks and McCafés in Germany, which have adapted well to Europe's coffeehouse culture.

To ask for "takeout" or "to-go" in German, you say *zum Mitnehmen* (tsoom MIT-nay-men). Many restaurants also offer a takeout menu. In larger German cities you will often see signs in English for "coffee to go."

Gibt es einen Schnellimbiß in der Nähe? *(gibt es EYE-nen shnell-IM-biss in dare NAY-uh):* Is there a snack stand (or fast-food place) nearby?

There is a wide variety of German fast food (*das Fast-Food*) that ranges from the simple *Currywurst* (KUHR-ree vurst) or *Dönerkebab* (DERN-er-kay-pop) or gyro stand to chains such as Burger King, McDonald's, Nordsee (fish), Pizza Hut, and Subway. In large cities like Berlin, you'll see the *Wurstmaxe*, a walking hot dog vendor "wearing" a small grill attached to a belt around his waist.

Additional German names for places to eat or drink include:

Asia-Imbiß
asia IM-biss
Asian snack, takeout

Bar
bahr
bar

Brauhaus/Bierstube
BROW-house/beer-SHTOO-buh
tavern specializing in beer

Café
kah-FAY
café, coffeehouse

Gasthaus/Gasthof/Gaststätte
GAHST-house/GAHST-hohf/
gahst-SHTET-tuh
small restaurant or inn with typical German cuisine

Imbiß
IM-biss
snack stand, fast food

Kneipe
k-NYPE-uh
bar, pub

Ratskeller
RAHTS-kel-ler
restaurant in the city hall

Restaurant
RES-tuh-rahn *or* RES-tuh-rahnt
restaurant

Weinstube	wine bar
vine-SHTOO-buh	
Wirtshaus	tavern, pub
VEERTS-howz	

 Wir gehen heute zum Chinesen. *(veer GAY-en HOY-tuh tsoom khee-NAY-zen):* Today we're going to a/the Chinese restaurant.

Although you should try it, you're certainly not limited to German cuisine, or *deutsche Küche* (DOY-chuh KEWKH-uh), in the German-speaking countries. In fact, one of the most popular simple fast foods in Germany, the *Dönerkebab* (DERN-er-kay-pop), also spelled *Dönerkebap*, or usually just *der Döner* (dare DERN-er), comes from Turkey. Adapted to German tastes in the 1970s, this grilled meat dish is served in pita bread with lettuce and various toppings. The German *Currywurst* (KUHR-ree vurst), a chopped-up hot dog sprinkled with curry powder, is usually served with ketchup and fries on a paper plate, but there are many regional variations. As in all European countries, in Germany you'll find a wide variety of food offerings in restaurants ranging from Italian to Indian, from McDonald's to Chinese.

When Germans talk about going to an ethnic food restaurant, they use *zum*-phrases like *zum Chinesen* (tsoom khee-NAY-zen), "to the Chinese restaurant," or *zum Italiener* (tsoom ee-TAHL-ee-AY-ner), "to the Italian restaurant." Note: Although you will find "Mexican" restaurants in many German cities, most of them serve food that, though perfectly good, has little if anything to do with Mexican cuisine. On the other hand, Asian, Greek, Italian, Turkish, and Indian food is more authentic, even if adapted somewhat to German tastes.

Wir essen heute chinesisch.	We're having Chinese (cuisine) today.
veer ES-sen HOY-tuh khee-NAYS-ish	

Wir essen italienisch.
veer ES-sen ee-TAHL-ee-AY-nish

We're eating Italian (cuisine).

 Wo ist die Toilette? *(voh ist dee toy-LET-tuh):* Where is the restroom?

The restroom in a restaurant or other establishment may also be marked *WC* (for "water closet"). Usually there are symbols for men or women on the door, but sometimes also the words *Damen* (ladies) and *Herren* (gentlemen/men). Some small cafés and bars in Germany actually charge a fee (usually about 50 euro cents) for using the toilet, even if you are a customer! Fortunately, this is a rare practice.

 Eine Speisekarte, bitte. *(EYE-nuh SHPY-zuh KAR-tuh BIT-tuh):* A menu, please.

By law, German restaurants are required to display their menu (*die Speisekarte*) outside, at, or near the entrance, so customers can see the prices and selection before they enter. Usually, you find your own table and seat yourself. A waiter may suggest a table, but there is almost never a host or hostess to seat you (and then usually only in expensive, exclusive restaurants).

The daily special in a German restaurant is called *das Menü* (dahs men-EW). It is a set menu with a combination of items at a special price. The regular menu in a restaurant is known as *die Speisekarte* (dee SHPYE-zuh-KAR-tuh).

To ask for a menu in English, say *Haben Sie eine Speisekarte auf Englisch?* (HAH-ben zee EYE-nuh SHPY-zuh-KAR-tuh owf AYNG-lish). Here is a question the waiter, *der Kellner* (dare KELL-ner), or waitress, *die Kellnerin* (dee KELL-ner-in), may ask you after you've looked at the menu (with possible replies):

Was möchten Sie trinken?   What would you like to drink?
vahs MERG-ten zee TRINK-en
Ich möchte Apfelsaft.   I'd like apple juice.
eekh MERG-tuh AHP-fel-zahft
Ich möchte Orangensaft.   I'd like orange juice.
eekh MERG-tuh or-RAHN-jhen zahft

 Ich möchte ein Helles. *(eekh MERG-tuh eyn HEL-less):* I'd like a pale beer. **Ein Dunkles, bitte.** *(eyn DOONK-less BIT-tuh):* A dark beer, please.

In Germany you rarely order just a beer, or *ein Bier* (eyn beer). With hundreds of breweries and thousands of types of beer ranging from light to dark, from sweet to bitter, and from ale to malt, you need to be a little more specific. You will usually get a local beer rather than a national brand like Beck's, Jever, Löwenbräu, or Spaten. If you like a traditional pale *Pilsner* (or *Pils*) or a dark malt (*Malzbier*), then ask for that. You can also get nonalcoholic beer. Ask for *alkoholfreies Bier* (AHL-ko-hohl-FRY-es beer).

Ein Radler (eyn RAHD-ler) is similar to what the British call a "shandy," a mixture of beer and a carbonated soft drink (usually lemon-lime). If you want a less common, dark-beer *Radler*, you should order *ein dunkles Radler* (eyn DOONK-less RAHD-ler). A *Radler* (*das Radler* in Germany; *der Radler* in Austria) can be self-made or bought as a commercial product sold in a bottle or can.

Ein Weizenbier, bitte.   . A wheat beer, please.
eyn VITES-en-beer BIT-tuh

Haben Sie eine Weinkarte? *(HAH-ben zee EYE-nuh VINE-kar-tuh):* Do you have a wine menu?

Beer is the beverage that most people associate with Germany, and for good reason, but German wines are also excellent, particularly the dry white wines from several German wine regions. Most German restaurants will have a good wine list with a variety of wines from France, Italy, California, and other wine regions. To ask for dry or sweet wine, use these terms: *trocken* (dry), *halbtrocken* (semidry), *lieblich* (sweet).

Haben Sie einen Wein aus der Gegend? HAH-ben zee EYE-nen vine ows dare GAY-ghent	Do you have a wine from this region?

 Welchen Wein empfehlen Sie? *(VELKH-en vine emp-FAY-len zee):* What wine do you recommend?

You will generally get a good wine if you ask for a recommendation. You can help narrow the choice down with phrases like these:

Ich möchte einen (trockenen) Rotwein. eekh MERG-tuh EYE-nen (TROCK-en-en) ROHT-vine	I'd like a (dry) red wine.
Ich möchte einen (halbtrockenen) Weißwein. eekh MERG-tuh EYE-nen (HALP-trock-en-en) vyce-vine	I'd like a (semidry) white wine.

Ich möchte eine Weinschorle, bitte. *(eekh MERG-tuh EYE-nuh VINE-shor-leh BIT-tuh):* I'd like a wine spritzer, please.

A popular, refreshing alternative to straight wine, especially in the summer, is the wine spritzer. Known as *ein Gespritzter* (eyn guh-SHPRITS-ter) in Austria and Switzerland, the typical spritzer is a 50/50 mixture of white wine and soda water (*Mineralwasser, Sodawasser*), but *die Schorle* (sometimes *das Schorle*) can also be made with red wine, or with apple juice (*Apfelschorle*) or some other fruit juice (*Saftschorle*) rather than wine.

 Wir hätten gern Sprudelwasser. *(veer HET-ten gehrn SHPROO-del VAHS-ser):* We'd like sparkling water.

If you ask for water in a German restaurant, it will be bottled *Mineralwasser* that you pay for, and most likely it will be carbonated unless you say otherwise. Some waiters will ask which one you prefer.

Ich hätte lieber stilles Wasser.   I'd prefer noncarbonated water.
eekh HET-tuh LEE-ber SHTILL-es
   VAHS-ser

 Ich hätte gern einen Kaffee. *(eekh HET-tuh gehrn EYE-nen kah-FAY):* I'd like (a cup of) coffee.

Germans have always been very proud of their coffee, but today there is a greater variety than ever before. Italian espresso remains popular, but the word *Kaffee* can mean many things, from "straight" coffee to Italian, Viennese, or Starbucks versions. In the German-speaking countries it is common to have an after-dinner coffee.

Einen Espresso?   An espresso?
EYE-nen es-PRES-so
Nein, bitte einen normalen Kaffee   No, a regular coffee with milk (and
   mit Milch (und Zucker).   sugar), please.
nine BIT-tuh EYE-nen nor-MAHL-en
   kah-FAY mitt milkh (oont TSOOK-er)

 Wir möchten eine Vorspeise bestellen. *(veer MERG-ten EYE-nuh FOR-shpy-zuh buh-SHTELL-en):* We would like to order an appetizer.

If you'd like an appetizer before the main course, you can get a soup or salad, and often certain other dishes, depending on the type of restaurant. The typical German restaurant "mixed salad" (*gemischter Salat*) is not the typical American lettuce-and-tomato salad with dressing, but a coleslawlike mixture of lettuce, shredded carrots, cucumbers, red cabbage, and a sweetish-tasting mayonnaise-type dressing. Some restaurants also have a salad bar where you can make your own salad and choose a dressing.

Ja, die Suppe, bitte.   Yes, the soup, please.
yah dee ZOOP-puh BIT-tuh
Ich hätte gern einen Salat.   I'd like a salad.
eekh HET-tuh gehrn EYE-nen
   sah-LAHT

Was empfehlen Sie heute? *(vahs emp-FAY-len zee HOY-tuh)*: What do you recommend today?

If you want to dive into the vast world of German and Austrian cuisine, including the many regional dishes, you may want to buy a special German-English menu guide or reader. The following are some typical items found on a German menu with accompanying phrases:

Ich möchte die Bachforelle. eekh MERG-tuh dee BAHKH-for-el-luh	I'd like the brook trout.

Wir nehmen das Hähnchen/
     Hendl.
 veer NAY-men dahs HEN-shen/
     HEN-del
	We'll have the (broiled) chicken.

Ich nehme die Rindsrouladen.
 eekh NAY-muh dee RINTS-roo-
     LAH-den
	I'll take the beef roulade (vegetables
	     wrapped in meat).

 Ich will das Steak. *(eekh vill dahs shtayk)*: I want the steak.

To get your steak cooked the way you want it, you say: *englisch* (AYNG-lish) for rare, *medium* (MAY-dee-oom) for medium, or *durchgebraten* (DURKH-guh-brah-ten) for well done.

Ich möchte das Wiener Schnitzel.
 eekh MERG-tuh dahs VEEN-er
     SHNIT-sel
	I'd like the breaded veal cutlet
	     (Viennese cutlet).

Was gibt es als Beilage? *(vahs gibt ess ahls BY-lah-guh):* What comes with that?

Although there are exceptions, most of the time German restaurants do not include a salad and a vegetable with the main dish you have ordered. Usually, you have to order your side dish(es), called *Beilage*, separately.

 Bitte mit Pommes frites. *(BIT-tuh mitt pohm frit):* With french fries, please.

The most popular German *Beilage* (side dish) is potatoes, prepared in many delicious ways: baked, boiled, fried, mashed, and so on. Other potato items on the menu might include:

Bratkartoffeln BRAHT-kar-tohf-eln	pan-fried potatoes
Kartoffelpüree kar-tohf-el-pew-ray	mashed potatoes
Pellkartoffeln pell-kar-tohf-eln	baked potatoes
Salzkartoffeln salts-kar-tohf-eln	boiled potatoes

 Was ist das? *(vahs ist dahs):* What is that?

If you're not sure what an item on the menu is, or what's in it, be sure to ask. If you want to know the ingredients, you ask:

Welche Zutaten sind drinnen? | What ingredients are in it?
VELKH-eh TSOO-tah-ten zint
   DRIN-nen

Ich kann nichts mit...essen. | I can't eat anything with . . .
eekh kahn nikhts mitt...ESS-en

Ich bin Vegetarier(in). | I'm a vegetarian (female vegetarian).
eekh bin vay-guh-TAH-reer(een)

Ich bin allergisch gegen... | I'm allergic to . . .
eekh bin ah-LEHRGH-ish GAY-gen

 Guten Appetit! *(GOO-ten ahp-puh-TEET):* Enjoy your meal!

This is usually said by the host when the food is served (at home or in a restaurant). However, in a restaurant it is common for people in the same party to be served at different times, depending on what they ordered from the menu. Rather than let the food get cold, it is perfectly OK to begin eating when you are served, but you may wish to ask: *Darf ich?* (darf eekh), or *May I?*

 Das ist nicht das, was ich bestellt habe. *(dahs ist nikht dahs vahs eek beh-STELLT HAH-buh):* That's not what I ordered.

Sometimes your steak is not cooked the way you ordered it, or you have mashed potatoes when you ordered fries. Here are some phrases for getting what you want:

Ich habe...bestellt. | I ordered . . .
eek HAH-buh...buh-SHTELLT

Das ist kalt. | This is cold.
dahs ist kahlt

Das ist gebrannt.	This is burnt.
dahs ist guh-BRAHNT	
Das ist versalzen.	This is too salty.
dahs ist fer-SALTS-en	

 Was gibt es als Nachtisch? *(vahs gibt es als NAHKH-tish):* What do you have for dessert?

Restaurant desserts tend to be light in Germany, but sometimes there can be a wide range of delicious and fattening choices, especially pastries. Here are a few possibilities:

Wir möchten den Apfelstrudel.	We'd like the apple strudel.
veer MERG-ten dane AHP-fel- SHTROO-del	
Ich will den Kompott.	I want the (stewed) fruit cup.
eekh vill dane kohm-POTE	
Ich möchte den Kuchen/die Torte.	I'd like the cake/tort.
eekh MERG-teh dane KOOKH-en/ dee TOR-tuh	
Ich nehme das Vanilleeis.	I'll have the vanilla ice cream.
eekh NAY-muh dahs vah-NEE-yuh-ice	

 Könnten wir Grappa haben? *(KERN-ten veer GRAHP-pa HAH-ben):* Could we have some grappa?

In Italian restaurants in Germany, the Italian national drink, grappa, a grape-based brandy (70 to 125 proof) is a common digestif (*der Digestif*), often served to regular customers "on the house" after their meal. Often guests have a choice of either grappa or Sambuca, an anise-flavored spirit (similar to Greek ouzo). Sambuca is usually served chilled in a shot glass with three coffee beans floating on top, representing health, happiness, and prosperity.

In almost any restaurant in German-speaking Europe you can order an after-dinner drink such as brandy (*Weinbrand*), cognac (*Cognac*), Jägermeister, port wine, or other spirits.

 Zahlen, bitte! *(TSALL-en BIT-tuh):* Check, please! (literally, "Pay, please!")

This is the most common phrase used to ask for the check in a restaurant. You can also say *Die Rechnung, bitte!* (dee REKH-noong BIT-tuh). In Europe it is considered impolite for the food server to bring the check before being asked. If you simply wait for the check, it may never come!

The procedures for paying the bill and tipping in German-speaking Europe are very different from those in the United States. You should not leave a tip on the table, American style. You will almost always settle the bill at the table with your food server, who carries cash and often these days a handheld digital device that displays your order and calculates the bill. Usually you round off the amount of the bill or add a few euros as *Trinkgeld* (a tip). When you don't want change back from the amount you handed the waiter or waitress, say:

Es stimmt so.   Keep the change.
ess shtimmt so

Chapter 9

Shopping for Food

 Gibt es einen Markt heute in der Stadt? *(gibt ess EYE-nen markt HOY-tuh in dare shtatt):* Is there a market in town today?

Large cities and small towns usually have a market square (or several) where farmers from the region sell their fresh produce and groceries on certain days. These colorful open-air markets are both a cultural treat and an opportunity to try some of the local foods. If you don't happen to stumble upon one, ask the locals when and where the market takes place. A typical town market fills a local square with booths and colorful displays of all kinds of produce, sausages, cheese, bread, oils and spices, wine, and other foods and beverages. Usually you'll also see many nonfood items as well, including flowers (*Blumen*) and arts and crafts.

Some markets are open only one or two days a week in season, while others are open daily all year round. Freiburg's classic *Münstermarkt* on the cathedral (*Münster*) square, for example, is open Monday through Friday from 7:00 A.M. until 1:00 P.M., and Saturday until 1:30 P.M. Berlin's *Wochenmarkt* (weekly market) actually takes place twice a week on the Karl-August-Platz, from 8:00 A.M. to 1:00 P.M. on

Wednesday and until 2:00 P.M. on Saturday. Large cities like Berlin, Frankfurt, or Munich have many open-air markets, with a few even held on Sunday.

Traditionally, there are many different kinds of markets. A *Bauern-markt* (BOW-ern-markt), farmers' market, or *Wochenmarkt* (VOKH-en-markt), weekly market, is mostly for food. A *Flohmarkt* (FLOW-markt), flea market, or *Trödelmarkt* (TRER-del-markt), which sells antiques or used goods, may have some food, but that's not the main attraction. Of course, beginning around December 1, you don't want to miss the many *Weihnachtsmärkte* (Christmas markets) that spring up all across Germany and the other German-speaking countries.

Unlike in some parts of Europe, bargaining is not really part of the German market experience. The price you see or the price you are told is the price you are expected to pay. If you want to buy in quantity or make some sort of deal for a particular (usually nonfood) item, you may suggest a lower price, but this is not the norm for an open-air food market. At a flea or antiques market, on the other hand, bargaining is more common and expected.

Ich möchte ein halbes Kilo davon.	I'd like half a kilo of that.
eekh MERG-tuh EYE-nuh HALB-es KEE-lo da-FON	
Ich nehme drei davon.	I'll take three of those.
eekh NAY-muh dry da-FON	
Wo finde ich Spargel und Spreewald-Gurken?	Where can I find asparagus and Spreewald pickles? (Berlin region)
voh FIN-duh eekh SHPAR-ghel oont SHPRAY-vahlt-GOORK-en	
Verkauft man hier Pilze?	Are there mushrooms for sale here?
fer-KOWFT mahn here PILTS-uh	

Gibt es einen Supermarkt in der Nähe? *(gibt ess EYE-nen SU-per-markt in dare NAY-uh):* Is there a supermarket near here?

German supermarkets are not unlike those in the United States, although they are usually a little smaller and offer a somewhat more limited selection of brand names and products. In big cities they are located all over town. In smaller towns one or two supermarkets may be located on the edge of town on what was once agricultural land. Unlike in the United States, most German department stores also have supermarkets, usually in the basement. (But Berlin's KaDeWe, the largest department store in continental Europe, has its large grocery and gourmet section on the top floor.) Some of the larger German supermarket chains are Aldi, Edeka, Kaiser's, Lidl, Plus, Real, Rewe, and Tengelmann.

Germans tend to shop daily for groceries in small local and neighborhood grocery stores (*Lebensmittelgeschäft*), especially for bread, fruit, produce, and other fresh items, but they also make weekly visits to a supermarket for bulk purchases and specialty items. Supermarkets offer lower prices and a larger selection. Many offer reward programs for regular shoppers.

Besides the normal produce, meat, and other departments, German supermarkets usually have a bakery/pastry section (*Bäckerei*), wine and other alcoholic beverages, a delicatessen (cheeses, meats, etc.), and a large newsstand. You can also find non-grocery items such as cosmetics, utensils, cookware, and household and paper products.

Like other German shops and stores, supermarkets are closed on Sunday. Usually they are open until 8:00 P.M. Monday through Saturday. In large cities they may not close until midnight, although some departments may close earlier. Some supermarkets in tourist areas may accept credit cards (look for the signs), but this is not very common. Small neighborhood grocery stores and markets almost never accept credit cards.

Bitte, wo finde ich die Weinabteilung? BIT-tuh voh FIN-duh eekh dee VINE-ahb-TYE-loong	Where can I find the wine section?
Können Sie mir bitte zeigen, wo ich Kaffee/Tee finde? KERN-nen zee mir BIT-tuh TSY-ghen voh eekh kah-FAY/tay FIN-duh	Can you please show me where I can find coffee/tea?
Ich brauche...Eier/Obst und Gemüse/Käse/Milch. eekh BROW-khuh ... EY-er/ohbst oont guh-MEW-zuh/ KAY-zuh/milkh	I need ... eggs/fruit and vegetables/ cheese/milk.

 Wo ist die Leergutabgabe? *(voh ist dee LEHR-goot-ahb-gah-buh):* Where is the bottle return?

Many beverages, from beer to soft drinks, are sold in glass or plastic return-deposit bottles (*Pfandflaschen*, PFAHNT-flah-shen) in Germany. Large supermarkets have automated bottle-return machines (*der Leergutautomat*) that scan the bottle labels and print out a receipt for the total amount due to you, which you then show to the cashier at checkout for payment. On weekends, there can be long lines of people returning their collection of deposit bottles. Smaller markets will also accept deposit bottles, but not in large quantities. (By law, you do not have to return bottles to the store that sold them.) You should remember not to just throw *Pfandflaschen* away! You have paid a deposit of between 8 to 25 euro cents per bottle, depending on the type of bottle (not all bottles have a deposit) that you want to get back.

 Wo sind die Einkaufswagen? *(voh sint dee EYN-kowfs-VAHG-en):* Where are the shopping carts?

Shopping carts in German and other European grocery stores require the deposit of a one-euro coin, which releases a security chain, so you can use the cart. You get your coin back when you return the cart and replace the security chain.

The smaller plastic baskets (*Korb*), sometimes with wheels and a handle that extends, are available in many supermarkets and drugstores for free, but they hold less than the metal carts.

 Eine Tüte, bitte. *(EYE-nuh TEW-tuh BIT-tuh):* A bag, please.

What an American will probably notice first at a European grocery store checkout stand (*die Kasse*) is that the clerk is sitting down. It's a good idea to bring your own shopping bag, since most grocery stores charge you for a cloth or plastic bag. (Paper is rarely an option.) Be prepared to quickly bag your own things, pay (usually cash), and move on. Europeans can be rather pushy at the checkout stand.

Eine Quittung, bitte.   A receipt, please.
EYE-nuh KVIT-toong BIT-tuh

Zwei Roggenbrote, bitte. *(tsvye ROG-gen-BROHT-uh BIT-tuh):* Two loaves of rye bread, please.

Germans love their bread, and they prefer it fresh out of the oven from the *Bäckerei* (BECK-er-eye), or bakery, just down the street. While the French may have their many cheese varieties, Germans pride themselves on the more than 200 types of bread they like to eat for breakfast and with other meals. From *Schwarzbrot* (brown bread) to *Roggenbrot* (rye bread), from *Brötchen* to *Semmeln* (the northern and southern German words, respectively, for bread rolls), *Brot* in German life takes on the literal meaning of "daily bread" (*tägliches Brot*).

American-style white bread is found in Germany only as *Toastbrot* (denser and better tasting than normal American white bread). German *Weißbrot* (VYCE-broht), white bread, is usually baked as a round or oval loaf (with a thick crust), in rolls, or as a French-style baguette. From crescent rolls, called *Hörnchen* (HERN-khen), to whole-grain loaves, or *Vollkornbrot* (FOLL-korn-broht), you'll want to try the many varieties and flavors of the delicious bread that comes from ovens in Austria, Germany, and Switzerland.

Although there are bakeries on almost every corner and in supermarkets in Germany, bread connoisseurs make a definite distinction between the chain-store bakeries with prepackaged doughs, and a genuine bakery with a highly trained *Bäckermeister* (certified master baker) who bakes his/her bread from scratch.

Haben Sie frische Schrippen?	Do you have fresh (Berlin-style) rolls?
HAH-ben zee FRISH-uh SHRIP-pen	
Ich möchte sechs Stück von den Kaisersemmeln.	I'd like six kaiser rolls.
eekh MERG-tuh zex shtewk fon dane KYE-zer-ZEM-meln	

Können Sie bitte das Brot schneiden?

KERN-nen zee BIT-tuh dahs broht SHNYE-den

Can you please slice the bread?

 Ist die Bäckerei sonntags geöffnet? *(ist dee BECK-er-eye SONN-tahgs guh-ERF-net)*: Is the bakery open on Sunday?

Bakeries in Germany are one of the few exceptions to shops being closed on Sunday. Since Germans also like fresh bread on Sunday, the local bakery is allowed to open on Sunday mornings (but not all of them do). A typical bakery is open weekdays from 6:30 A.M. until 6:30 P.M., and Saturday until 1:30 P.M. Some are also open from 7:00 to 10:00 A.M. on Sunday, but may be closed on a Monday or some other day. Bakeries combined with a *Konditorei* (pastry shop) or a small café can have opening hours similar to a restaurant.

 Ein Kilo Weißwurst, bitte. *(eyn KEE-loh VYCE-voorst BIT-tuh)*: One kilo (2.2 lbs) of the white sausage, please.

A butcher shop is known by two different names in German, depending on the region. The most common term is *Fleischerei* (FLY-sher-eye), but in southern Germany, Switzerland, and parts of Austria, a butcher shop is a *Metzgerei* (METS-gher-eye). A *Fleischer* or *Metzger* (butcher) prepares meats, poultry, and sausages; puts them on display; and sells them to customers who want their meat products handled by a professional. Supermarkets also have a meat department headed by a *Fleischer* or *Fleischerin*.

If you also like fish (*Fisch*) and seafood (*Meeresfrüchte*), look for a fishmonger (*Fischhändler*) or a seafood shop where fresh seafood is available. Some supermarkets also have good fish and seafood departments with fresh and frozen seafood.

Haben Sie Westfälischen Schinken?	Do you have Westphalian ham?
HAH-ben zee vest-FEHL-ish-en SHINK-en	
Können Sie mir ein Kilo Rindfleisch geben?	Could you give me a kilo of beef?
KERN-nen zee meer eyn KEE-loh RINT-flysh GAY-ben	
Ich hätte gern vier Stück Hühnerbrust.	I'd like four chicken breasts.
eekh HET-tuh gehrn feer shtewk HEW-ner-broost	
Ich möchte fünf Scheiben Leberwurst.	I'd like five slices of liverwurst.
eekh MERG-tuh fewnf SHY-ben LAY-ber-voorst	

 Sind das Bio-Kirschen? *(zint dahs BEE-oh-KIRSH-en):* Are those organically grown cherries?

Germany has many *Bioläden* (BEE-oh-LAY-den) and even *Biosupermärkte* (Alnatura and Basic are two) that sell only organically grown fruits, vegetables, and other foods. But you can also find *Bio* (BEE-oh) products being sold at regular grocery stores, green grocers, and at open-air markets. Many small neighborhood grocery stores in Germany feature a colorful outdoor storefront display of fruits and vegetables (*Obst und Gemüse*), where you can select what looks good to you. With the extensive produce offerings of supermarkets and regular grocery stores, a separate green grocer or produce shop (*Gemüseladen*) is more difficult to find in Germany these days, but there are still some around.

Wie viel kosten die Bananen?   How much are the bananas?
vee feel KOST-en dee bah-NAHN-en

Haben Sie frische Trauben heute?   Do you have fresh grapes today?
HAH-ben zee FRISH-uh TROW-ben
    HOY-tuh

Ich suche Koriander.   I'm looking for cilantro (coriander).
eekh ZOOKH-uh KOHR-ee-AHN-dare

 Was kostet ein Pfund... *(vahs KOST-et eyn pfoont):* What does a (metric) pound of . . . cost?

Like other Europeans, Germans use the metric system of weights and measures. But the old German unit known as *das Pfund* is still used by sellers and buyers of groceries. A German *Pfund* is 500 grams or a half kilogram (1.1 lbs). You may see signs in Germany that price things in pounds, but just remember it is a metric pound (500 grams).

 Ich möchte ein Erdbeereis. *(eekh MERG-tuh eyn AIRT-bare-ice):* I'd like some strawberry ice cream.

In Germany in the summer the temperatures can get to the point that cooling off with some ice cream, *das Eis* (dahs ice), seems like a very good idea. If you want an ice-cream cone, ask for *eine Tüte* (EYE-nuh TEW-tuh). Scoops of ice cream are called *Kugeln* (KOOG-eln). If you want two scoops, ask for *zwei Kugeln*; one scoop is *eine Kugel*. In a dish you can ask for *eine Portion* (EYE-nuh POR-tsee-ohn) or *zwei Portionen.*

Ice cream—in a cone; a cup, called *Becher* (BEKH-er); or a dish, a *Schale* (SHAH-luh)—is sold at ice-cream stands, in a *Konditorei* (sometimes at a special ice-cream window in the summer), or in an ice-cream parlor, called either *Eiscafé* (ice-kah-FAY) or *Eisdiele* (ice-DEE-luh).

The standard flavors are vanilla, called *Vanille* (vah-NEE-yuh); *Erdbeere* (AIRT-bare-uh) for strawberry; and *Schokolade* (show-koh-LAH-duh), chocolate; but there are many others, from *Ananas* (ahn-uh-nahs, pineapple) to *Zitrone* (tsee-TROH-nuh, lemon). A popular dish is *ein gemischtes Eis* (eyn guh-MISH-tes ice), a mix of chocolate, strawberry, and vanilla ice cream served in a dish or bowl with a wafer and (optional) whipped cream on top.

Welche Geschmackssorten haben Sie?	What flavors do you have?
VELKH-uh guh-SHMAHKS-sort-en HAH-ben zee	
Haben Sie Joghurteis?	Do you have frozen yogurt?
HAH-ben zee YO-gurt-ice	
Ich möchte einen Becher Himbeereis.	I'd like a cup of raspberry ice cream.
eekh MERG-tuh EYE-nen BEKH-er HIM-bare-ice	

Chapter 10

Entertainment and Leisure Time

 Gehen wir ins Kino! *(GAY-en veer ins KEE-noh)*: Let's go to the movies!

Most of the movies, called *Filme* (FILM-uh), that Germans and Austrians watch come from Hollywood, but they are dubbed, or *synchronisiert* (ZIN-kron-uh-zeert), in German. In German Switzerland English-language films normally run with the original sound and German subtitles. Of course, German-language films made in Austria, Germany, or Switzerland also play in *Kinos* (KEE-nohz), or cinemas, and multiplexes, but they make up only about 10 percent of the total each year. In larger German cities there are cinemas that show Hollywood and other English-language films in the original version, with the English soundtrack and usually no German subtitles. The abbreviations used in newspaper or online movie listings are *OmU* for movies with German subtitles and *OF, OV,* or *O-Ton* for movies in the original language without subtitles.

Was läuft im Kino?	What's playing at the movies?
vahs loyft im KEE-noh	
Wer spielt in dem Film?	Who's in the movie?
vehr shpeelt in dame film	
Wann beginnt der Film?	When does the film start?
vahn be-GINNT dare film	

 Wie viel kostet eine Kinokarte? *(vee feel KOST-et EYE-nuh KAR-tuh):* How much is a movie ticket?

As in most parts of the world, German cinemas, especially in big cities, have largely become multiscreen cineplexes, but there are still many traditional and art-house movie theaters. The cost of admission to a German cinema is about the same as in the United States.

Haben Sie diesen Film schon gesehen?	Have you already seen this movie?
HAH-ben zee DEE-zen film shohn guh-ZAY-en	
Ich habe diesen Film nicht/schon gesehen.	I haven't/I've already seen this movie.
eek HAH-buh DEE-zen film nikht/ shohn guh-ZAY-en	
Der Film hat mir (gut) gefallen.	I (really) liked the movie.
dare film haht meer (goot) guh-FALL-en	
Der Film hat mir (gar) nicht gefallen.	I (really) didn't like the movie.
dare film haht meer (gar) nikht guh-FALL-en	

Was gibt es heute Abend im Fernsehen? *(vahs gibt ess HOY-tuh AH-bent im FEHRN-zay-en):* What's on TV tonight?

In hotel or guest rooms in German-speaking Europe you will usually have cable TV that includes English-language channels such as CNN International or BBC World. But television *auf Deutsch* is an excellent way to learn German, especially when you watch familiar U.S. and British TV series or game shows in their German versions. If you'd like to watch some TV in German, here are some things to know:

The two main German public television networks are ARD (ah-air-day), also called *das Erste* (dahs AIR-stuh), "the First"; and ZDF (tsett-day-eff), which stands for *Zweites Deutsches Fernsehen* (TSVYE-tes DOY-chess FEHRN-zay-en), or "Second German TV." Larger German cities usually have what is called a "third channel" that broadcasts local and regional news and weather, as well as additional entertainment, cultural, and political programming. Germany also has several private TV networks (*Sender*), including RTL, RTL II, Pro Sieben, Sat 1, and Vox. It is on these commercial TV channels that you'll find most of the American shows (dubbed in German). Note: The German television standard (PAL) and Region 2 DVDs are not compatible with the American (ATSC/NTSC) system and Region 1 DVDs.

Wo ist das Fernsehprogramm?	Where is the TV schedule/guide?
voh ist dahs FEHRN-zay-pro-GRAM	
Welche Sendung empfehlen Sie?	What show do you recommend?
VELKH-uh ZEN-doong	
emp-FAY-len zee	

Wann ist das Fußballspiel/Tennisspiel? *(vahn ist dahs FOOS-ball-shpeel/TEN-nis-shpeel):* When is the soccer/tennis game?

Another good option on German TV is soccer and other sporting events, because it's not necessary for you to fully understand the commentary in order to follow the game. See Chapter 15, "Sports," for more.

Wer spielt?	Who's playing? (What team is playing?)
vehr shpeelt	
Wie steht's?	What's the score?
vee shtayts	

 Gehen wir ins Konzert. *(GAY-en veer ins kohn-SERT):* Let's go to a/the concert.

Any large German city or town offers a great variety of entertainment ranging from nightclubs and discos to concerts, museums, and live theater.

Wohin heute Abend?	Where to tonight?
voh-hin HOY-tuh AH-bent	

 Gehen wir ins Spielcasino. *(GAY-en veer ins SHPEEL-kah-SEE-noh):* Let's go to a casino.

Most large German cities and some resorts have gambling casinos usually for tourists only. Local residents are not allowed to gamble there. Other entertainment possibilities might include:

Gehen wir in die Oper.	Let's go to the opera.
GAY-en veer in dee OH-per	

Gehen wir in einen Tanzclub.   Let's go to a dance club.
GAY-en veer in EYE-nen
  TAHNTS-kloob

Gehen wir in einen Technoclub.   Let's go to a techno club.
GAY-en veer in EYE-nen
  TECH-no-kloob

Gehen wir ins Theater.   Let's go to the theater/a play.
GAY-en veer ins tay-OT-ter

 Gibt es ein Kurbad in der Nähe? *(gibt ess eyn KOOR-baht in dare NAY-uh):* Is there a spa nearby?

The German word *Bad* (baht) can mean either bath or spa. German towns like Baden-Baden and Bad Kreuznach got their names from the Roman baths that were once located there, and in many cases still are. "Taking the waters" (*eine Kur machen*) remains a popular German custom; in fact, such a *Kur* can be paid for by a German health plan. Though your own health plan may not cover this, consider a visit to one of Germany's many relaxing indoor and natural outdoor spas.

 Ich möchte ein Fitnesscenter besuchen. *(eekh MERG-tuh eyn FIT-ness-CEN-ter beh-ZOOKH-en):* I'd like to visit a gym/fitness studio.

Today, more and more Germans go to a gym or fitness studio (*das Fitnesscenter* or *das Fitnessstudio*) for a workout (*der Work-out*) with a *Fitnesstrainer* several times a week. In stark contrast to the traditional *Sportverein* gym of old, McFit is a successful German chain of budget health studios (founded in 1997) offering modern workout facilities with its own special training program. (Atypical for Germany, the

McFit studios are open 24/7.) Almost any German town of even moderate size has several commercial fitness centers. The Pilates fitness program was first developed by the German Joseph Hubert Pilates while he was a POW in England during World War I.

Was kostet es pro Stunde/Tag/ Woche?	How much is it per hour/day/week?
vahs KOST-et ess pro SHTOON-duh/ tahg/VOHK-uh	
Wie werde ich Mitglied?	How do I become a member?
vee VEHR-da eekh MIT-gleet	

 Haben Sie ein Hobby? *(HAH-ben zee eyn HOB-bee):* Do you (formal) have a hobby?

Germans have a wide range of hobbies and interests. These would include: *Basteln* (BAHS-teln), or arts and crafts; *Fotografie* (fo-toh-grah-FEE), photography; *Gärtnerei* (GEHRT-nare-eye), or gardening; *Kochen* (KOKH-en), or cooking; and *Malen* (MAH-len), or painting.

Ich fotografiere gern.	I like to take photos.
eekh fo-toh-gra-FEER-uh gehrn	
Ich sammle Briefmarken/Münzen.	I collect stamps/coins.
eekh ZAHM-luh BREEF-mark-en/ MEWN-tsen	
Mein Hobby ist Briefmarken- sammeln.	My hobby is stamp collecting.
myne HOB-bee ist BREEF-mark-en- ZAHM-meln	

Spielst du Schach? *(shpeelst doo shahkh):* Do you play chess? (familiar)

To ask someone if he/she plays a game, sport, or musical instrument, use one of these two phrases: *Spielst du...?* (familiar) or *Spielen Sie...?* (formal), followed by the name of the game, sport, or instrument.

Spielen Sie Tennis?	Do you play tennis? (formal)
SHPEEL-en zee TEN-nis	
Spielst du Gitarre?	Do you play (the) guitar? (familiar)
shpeelst doo guh-TAHR-uh	

 Nein, aber ich spiele Klavier. *(nyne AH-ber eekh SHPEEL-uh klah-VEER):* No, but I play (the) piano.

To tell someone what you play, you use the pronoun *ich*.

Ich spiele Computerspiele.	I play computer games.
eekh SHPEEL-uh kohm-POO-ter- SHPEEL-uh	
Ich spiele Karten.	I play cards.
eekh SHPEEL-uh KAR-ten	
Ich spiele Dame.	I play checkers/draughts.
eekh SHPEEL-uh DAH-muh	

 Wo ist das Verkehrsamt? *(voh ist dahs fer-KEHRS-ahmt):* Where's the tourist office?

Time to see the sights! The local tourist office has maps and brochures for the local sights, and can often help you find hotel, pension, B&B, or hostel accommodations. The tourist office is often marked with a white *I* (for *Informationen*) in a blue circle. Almost any Austrian, German, or Swiss town or region has many wonderful historical and scenic things to see. In most cases, the staff people in tourist offices speak English, but here are a few useful sightseeing phrases:

Was gibt es hier zu sehen?
What is there to see here?
vahs gibt ess here tsoo ZAY-en

Gibt es eine Führung auf
Is there a guided tour in English?
   Englisch?
gibt ess EYE-nuh FEWR-oong owf
   AYNG-lish

Wir möchten den Dom/das
We'd like to see the cathedral/
   Schloss sehen.
     the castle.
veer MERG-ten dane dome/dahs
   shlohss ZAY-en

Wie viel kostet der Eintritt?
How much is admission?
vee feel KOST-et dare EYN-tritt

Darf man fotografieren?
Is it all right to take photos?
darf mahn fo-toh-grah-FEER-en

Chapter 11

Museums and Memorials

 Gehen wir ins Museum. *(GAY-en veer ins moo-ZAY-oom):* Let's go to a/the museum.

Germany is a nation of museums! You will find many kinds of museums and art galleries in cities and small towns all across Germany, Austria, and Switzerland. Besides the numerous comprehensive historical and art museums found in larger cities, almost every region and small town also has its own *Heimatmuseum* (HY-maht-moo-ZAY-oom) featuring the local history and traditions. Most of them are very interesting and well worth a visit. In addition, there are the specialty museums—for everything from clocks to toys. There are museums for every interest and taste. In Berlin, Frankfurt, Munich, Vienna, Zurich, and other large cities in German-speaking Europe, you could spend weeks visiting a new museum every day.

Some German museums offer free admission on certain days (usually Sunday) or at certain times (after 7:00 P.M., for example). Many museums and some tourist attractions are closed on Monday, but this varies.

Wann ist das Museum geschlossen?	When is the museum closed?
vahn ist dahs moo-ZAY-oom guh-SHLOHS-sen	
Ist das ein Kunsthistorisches Museum?	Is that an art history museum?
ist dahs eyn KOONST-hiz-TOR-ish-es moo-ZAY-oom	
Ich möchte ein Kunstmuseum besichtigen.	I'd like to visit an art museum.
eekh MERG-tuh eyn koonst-moo-ZAY-oom buh-ZEEKH-tee-ghen	
Moderne oder klassische Kunst?	Modern or classic art?
moh-DARE-nuh OH-dare KLAHSS-ish-uh koonst	

 Ich bin Student/Studentin. *(eekh bin shtoo-DENT/shtoo-DENT-in):* I'm a student. (male/female)

Most museums and other attractions in Europe offer a special discounted student rate, but you usually need to present proof that you are a student, such as an international student I.D. card, called a *Studentenausweis* (shtoo-DENT-en-OWS-vyce), to be admitted at the student rate. You can get an International Student Identity Card (ISIC) from the ISIC Association. The card also offers other travel-related discounts. See www.isic.org for details.

Wo ist die Garderobe? *(voh ist dee GAR-duh-ROH-buh)*: Where is the checkroom/coatroom?

Most museums have a checkroom where you are invited (or required) to leave backpacks, heavy coats, cameras (if no photography is allowed), and other articles before entering the exhibit area. There is usually no charge for this service.

 Wo befindet sich das Jüdische Museum in Berlin? *(voh buh-FIN-det zeekh dahs YEW-dish-uh moo-ZAY-oom in bare-LEEN)*: Where is Berlin's Jewish Museum located?

The Jewish Museum in Berlin (www.jmberlin.de) opened to the public in 2001. Berlin's original Jewish museum, on Oranienburger Straße near today's restored Jewish synagogue, was founded in 1933, but was closed down by the Nazis in 1938. The new museum is notable for its radical *Blitz* (lightning bolt) modern design, in stark contrast to the baroque museum building to which it is attached. Polish-American architect Daniel Libeskind's design features underground passages connecting the museum's three main spaces representing Continuity with German History, Emigration from Germany, and the Holocaust. Located at Lindenstraße 9–14, the museum is open daily (even Mondays) and closes only for Christmas Eve, Rosh Hashanah, and Yom Kippur.

Wer hat das Holocaust-Denkmal entworfen? *(vehr haht dahs HO-lo-caust-DENK-mahl ent-VORF-en):* Who designed the Holocaust Memorial?

After a contentious, controversial start and years of debate, Berlin's Holocaust Memorial, dedicated to Europe's murdered Jews, now spreads out across a 19,000-square-meter (4.7-acre) city block located across the street from the new U.S. Embassy building, next to the Tiergarten park, and only a short walk south from the Brandenburg Gate. Completed in May 2005, the monument's vast field of 2,711 tomblike stelae forms a fascinating irregular pattern of light and shadow. You can only truly experience the memorial by walking into and within it. One striking feature of New York architect Peter Eisenman's design is the complete absence of names and specific symbols in the vast aboveground part of the memorial. Visitors strolling through the stelae will see no inscriptions, no triangles, no Stars of David, and no outright statement of the memorial's purpose. The architect's effort at abstraction and universality has been both condemned and praised, but he has stated that he did not want the stelae "turned into a graveyard" by adding names.

Many visitors overlook the rather-well-hidden underground *Ort der Information* (Place of Information) exhibit that is part of the Memorial to the Murdered Jews of Europe (*Denkmal für die ermordeten Juden Europas*), the Holocaust memorial's full name, and contains the names of all known Jewish Holocaust victims.

Wie komme ich zum Deutschen Museum? *(vee KOHM-muh eekh tsoom DOYT-chen moo-ZAY-oom):* How do I get to the Deutsches Museum?

Munich's *Deutsches Museum* (German Museum) is a unique collection of science and technology, similar to the Smithsonian science and technology museums in Washington, DC. Standing on an island in the Isar River, the Deutsches Museum was founded in 1903 and displays machines, computers, automobiles, airplanes, and many other inventions from early times to the present day. The myriad exhibits on the many floors of the museum cannot all be seen in a single visit. Although it is named the "German Museum" and features many items from German scientists and inventors, the Deutsches Museum is also devoted to non-German technology. The museum's permanent exhibits include aerospace, ceramics, mathematics, metallurgy, music, printing technology, and much more. The new Museum of Transportation (*Deutsches Museum Verkehrszentrum*) branch of the Deutsches Museum in the Theresienhöhe district of Munich, which opened in 2003, allowed the museum to greatly expand its exhibit of motor vehicles and trains. There are also two other branches of the museum, one in Bonn, and another north of Munich at Oberschleißheim Airfield for aircraft too large to be displayed at the main museum. Chicago's Museum of Science and Industry was modeled after the Deutsches Museum. See www.deutsches-museum.de for more information (in English and German).

Chapter 12
Emergency German

 Achtung! *(AHK-toong):* Attention!/Caution!

This is the standard way of getting someone's attention in German. It almost always means that what comes next is urgent or important. It could be anything, from an announcement that your train will arrive late to a serious warning of danger. A similar word is *Vorsicht!*

Being aware of your surroundings is always a good idea, but what if you are unable to understand an important warning or a sign that says *Notausgang* (Emergency exit)? For safety reasons, it is important to know some of the common warnings in German. The following sections will provide you with some important warning phrases.

Vorsicht!   Caution!
FOR-zeekht

 Gefahr! *(guh-FAHR):* Danger!

In your travels through German-speaking countries, you may also see or hear:

Gefährlich!	Dangerous!
guh-FAIR-leekh	
Lebensgefahr!	Mortal danger!
LAY-bens-guh-fahr	
Feuer!	Fire!
FOY-er	

 Gift/giftig! *(gift/gif-teeg)*: Poison/poisonous!

This is a German "false friend"—don't be fooled by it! A "gift" or "present" in German is *das Geschenk* (das guh-SHENK). (For another false friend, see *Not* in the following section.)

Hilfe!	Help!
HILF-uh	
Hochspannung!	High voltage!/High tension!
hoke-SHPAH-noong	

 Es ist ein Notfall! *(ess ist eyn NOTE-fall)*: It's an emergency!

The German word or prefix *Not-* (pronounced like "note") does not mean "not"! When you see *Not-* on warning signs, it means "emergency," as in the following:

Notausgang	emergency exit
NOTE-OWS-gahng	
Notrufsäule	emergency call box
NOTE-roof-SOY-luh	

Rauchen verboten! *(ROWE-ken fair-BOH-ten):* No smoking!

The German word *verboten* (forbidden) is usually seen in combination with something that is prohibited. *Rauchen verboten* signs are not new, but Germans are being made increasingly aware of the dangers of smoking, often by new laws. Unheard of only a decade ago, the no-smoking zones in restaurants recently gave way to a law prohibiting any smoking in German restaurants at all. Smoking in public areas, such as train stations, is now also prohibited.

 Rufen Sie die Polizei! *(ROOF-en zee dee POLE-eet-sye):* Call the police!

While North America uses 911 and the United Kingdom 999 (or 112), in Germany and most of Europe the emergency phone number (*Notruf-nummer*) is 112. An emergency call to the police (*die Polizei*), fire department (*die Feuerwehr*), or for medical assistance (*der Rettungs-dienst*) is supposed to be possible via a single coordinated number throughout the European Union, but in practice this is not always the case. Although 112 can now be used in the German-speaking countries, the following alternate, traditional numbers are also used:

	Germany	Austria	Switzerland
Polizei (police)	110	133	117
Feuerwehr (fire dept.)	112	122	118
Rettungsdienst/Notarzt (medical emergency)	112	144	144

Rufen Sie einen Arzt! *(ROOF-en zee EYE-nen ahrtst):*
Call a doctor!

Along the autobahn and in train stations (including public transit) you will find emergency call boxes called *Notrufsäulen* (*NOTE-roof-soy-len*). Sometimes labeled *Notruf,* these red or orange-colored boxes allow you to directly contact the authorities in an emergency by picking up the receiver and/or pressing a call button.

 Rufen Sie einen Rettungswagen! *(ROOF-en zee EYE-nen RET-tungs-VAG-en):* Call an ambulance!

Depending on the region or the city, the German-speaking countries have two main emergency organizations that respond to medical emergency calls. The *Johanniter* (Order of Saint John, Protestant) and the *Malteser* (Order of Malta, Catholic), known collectively as the *Knights Hospitaller,* are the best-known nonprofit, religious German EMT organizations, both with a long history dating to the Crusades. Most municipalities also have their own emergency responders who are part of the fire department (*Feuerwehr*). When you see an ambulance responding to a medical emergency in German-speaking Europe, it may have the words *Johanniter, Malteser,* or *Feuerwehr* on it. Known since the 1950s officially as the *Johanniter-Unfall-Hilfe e.V.* and the *Malteser Hilfsdienst e.V.,* each of the two religious organizations has its own coat of arms and cross symbol, reflecting its historical background, but the responding personnel are trained in modern medical technology. There are also services provided by the German Red Cross (DRK), the *Samariter* (like the *Johanniter*), and the German Lifesaving Society (DLG). Any one of these rescue services may respond to a 112 emergency call, depending on the location and circumstances.

Ein Unfall ist passiert.	There's been an accident.
eyn OON-fall ist pah-SEERT	
Es gibt Schwerverletzte.	There are seriously injured people.
ess gibt shver-fer-LETS-tuh	
Haben Sie ein Handy?	Do you have a cell/mobile phone?
HAH-ben zee eyn HAHN-dee	

 Rufen Sie die Feuerwehr! *(ROOF-en zee dee FOY-er-vehr):* Call the fire department!

Firefighters in Germany and Europe are usually part of a city's or town's professional fire brigade (*Berufsfeuerwehr*), but there are also volunteer fire brigades (*Freiwillige Feuerwehr*) in small towns and rural areas. Private companies and factories may also have their own fire departments. Any German city with 100,000 or more inhabitants by law must have paid firefighters. Berlin has Germany's oldest municipal fire department (founded in 1851), with about 3,900 employees.

 Wo ist die nächste Polizeiwache? *(voh ist dee NEX-tuh POLE-eet-sye-VAKH-uh):* Where is the nearest police station?

Larger cities have a number of police precincts (*Polizeiabschnitte*) in addition to the main police headquarters (*Polizeipräsidium*). Berlin has just under forty police precinct stations.

 Ich bin (sehr) krank. *(eekh bin [zehr] krahnk):* I am (very) ill.

If you have a serious medical problem, you can go to a *Klinik* or *Kran-kenhaus* (both mean hospital) for an emergency. For minor problems, the German *Apotheke* (ah-poh-TAY-kuh), or pharmacy, is often all you need. The pharmacist (*Apotheker/Apothekerin*) will either sell you the appropriate medication or instruct you to see a doctor first.

Er/Sie ist sehr krank.	He/She is very ill.
air/zee ist zehr krahnk	
Es ist dringend!	It's urgent!
ess ist DRING-ent	
Ich brauche/Wir brauchen	I/We need a doctor.
einen Arzt.	
eekh BROW-kuh/veer BROW-ken	
EYE-nen ahrtst	

 Er/Sie muss ins Krankenhaus! *(air/zee mooss ins KRAHNK-en-house)*: He/She has to go to a hospital!

Germany has good public and private hospitals, even in smaller communities. In larger cities there is usually an emergency ward (*die Notaufnahme*) for accidents and injuries. Ask:

Wo ist die Notaufnahme?	Where is the emergency room/
voh ist dee NOTE-owf-NAHM-uh	reception?

 Hier tut es weh. *(here toot ess vay)*: Here's where it hurts.

This answers the following question:

Wo tut es weh?	Where does it hurt?
voh toot ess vay	

Chapter 13

Health Issues

 Ich möchte einen Termin machen. *(eekh MERG-tuh EYE-nen tehr-MEEN MAHKH-en):* I'd like to make an appointment.

Other than possible language difficulties, making a doctor's appointment in Germany is usually easier and quicker than in the United States. In most cases, you will be able to see the doctor the next day or within just a few days, even if you are a new patient. (Try doing that in the United States!) Doctors in Germany often have one weekday (usually Wednesday, *Mittwoch*) with limited (half-day) office hours (*Sprechstunden*). If you need to find a doctor, a pharmacist (*Apotheker/Apothekerin*) may be able to recommend one. If you really want an English-speaking doctor, you can contact the nearest U.S. consular office or the embassy in Berlin for a list of recommended physicians. (You can also check on the Internet at germany.usembassy.gov/acs/lists.html.) Another option is to look in the local Yellow Pages (*Gelbe Seiten*) under *Ärzte* (the Yellow Pages are also online at www.gelbeseiten.de). Although the doctor may speak some English, the office assistant (*Arzthelferin*) rarely does. As in the United States, a general practitioner (*allgemeine Medizin*) can refer you to a specialist (*Facharzt*), if needed.

If you have an urgent medical emergency, see the chapter Emergency German.

Wo ist Ihre Praxis?   Where is your office?
voh ist EAR-uh PRAHX-is

 Ich fühle mich nicht wohl. *(eekh FEW-luh meekh nikht vohl)*: I'm not feeling well.

If you are in pain, usually you can point or indicate in some way where it hurts. For more general, vague symptoms, however, it may be more difficult to communicate in German. For a complete diagnosis, the physician may want to get some X-rays, or *Röntgen* (RERNT-ghen), named for the German scientist Wilhelm Conrad Röntgen, who discovered them.

Mir ist schlecht.   I'm feeling queasy/nauseous.
meer ist shlekht
Ich habe mich (zweimal)   I threw up (twice).
  übergeben.
eekh HAH-buh meekh (TSVYE-mahl)
  EW-ber-GAY-ben
Ich habe Fieber.   I have a fever.
eekh HAH-buh FEE-ber
Hier tut es weh.   It hurts here.
here toot ess vay

Ich habe keinen Appetit.   I have no appetite.
eekh HAH-buh KY-nen
   ahp-puh-TITT

 Ich bin Diabetiker. *(eekh bin dee-ah-BET-ee-ker):* I'm diabetic.

If you have a preexisting or chronic condition, you may want to learn the German vocabulary related to it and make sure your health insurance will cover you during your stay in Europe. Some other health-related possibilities might include:

Ich bin im dritten Monat   I'm three months pregnant.
   schwanger.
eekh bin im DRIT-ten MO-naht
   SHVAHN-gair

Ich bin allergisch gegen...   I'm allergic to . . .
eekh bin ah-LEHRG-ish GAY-ghen

Ich bin Epileptiker(in).   I'm epileptic.
eekh bin ep-ee-LEP-tee-ker(in)

Ich habe Herzbeschwerden.   I have a heart condition.
eekh HAH-buh HAIRTS-buh-
   SHVEHR-den

 Ich brauche einen Zahnarzt. *(eekh BROW-khuh EYE-nen TSAHN-artst):* I need a dentist.

Dental care in Germany is generally very good, with modern technology and well-trained dentists. As with doctors, you can find a dentist through the consulate, embassy, or in the local Yellow Pages (*Gelbe Seiten*) under *Zahnärzte* or *Zahnmedizin* (remember: the Yellow Pages are also found online at www.gelbeseiten.de).

Dieser Zahn tut weh.	This tooth hurts.
DEE-zer tsahn toot vay	
Eine Plombe ist herausgefallen.	I've lost a filling.
EYE-nuh PLOHM-buh ist hare-OWSS-	
guh-FALL-en	

 Ich bin Privatpatient/Privatpatientin. *(eekh bin pree-VAHT-paht-see-ent/pree-VAHT-paht-see-en-tin):* I am a private patient (male/female).

If you go to a physician, dentist, or hospital (*Krankenhaus*) for treatment in Germany, you will have to pay the bill yourself (unless you are a citizen of Germany or the EU with health insurance). Since the insurance reform law of 2007, all persons living in Germany (citizens and foreign residents) must have health insurance. About 90 percent of Germans are covered by one of Germany's public, nonprofit *Krankenkassen* ("sickness funds," or public health insurers), with the rest having private health insurance. Only persons with an annual income exceeding a set minimum amount are eligible for private insurance.

You, as a tourist or visitor in Germany (for up to 90 days), are not required to have health insurance, but it is a very good idea! However, even if you do have insurance, you usually must pay the doctor or hospital yourself and then get reimbursed by your insurance plan. Even if your U.S. health insurance plan covers you in Europe, most German health-care providers will not accept it, and will ask for payment from you, the patient. You can also get short-term travel health coverage from an American or European insurance company, but in most cases, you will still have to pay the bill yourself first and then send it to your insurance company for reimbursement. (This also applies to Germans with private health insurance.) Also note that most German doctors and hospitals do not accept credit card payment, but they will usually agree to send you an invoice (sometimes even to your U.S. address!).

Americans or Canadians planning to stay in Germany for a period longer than 90 days must obtain a residence visa. In order to get a German residence visa, you have to show proof of health insurance, either through your employer or a private insurance company.

Können Sie mir etwas verschreiben?	Could you prescribe something for me?
KERN-nen zee meer ET-vahs fer-SHRYE-ben	
Wann soll ich wiederkommen?	When do you want me to come back?
vahn zoll eekh VEE-dare-KOHM-men	

 Wo ist die nächste Apotheke? *(voh ist dee NEX-tuh ah-po-TAY-kuh)*: Where is the nearest pharmacy?

Once you have a doctor's prescription, take it to a pharmacy (*Apotheke*). Most German pharmacies can be identified by a large red stylized *A* sign. (The green-theme, Dutch-based DocMorris discount pharmacy chain has recently introduced more competition into Germany's highly regulated pharmacy market, and does not use the *A* logo.) Note that even nonprescription medicines (*rezeptfreie Medikamente*), including aspirin and cold medicines, that you can buy in any grocery store in the United States will only be found in an *Apotheke* in Germany.

Haben Sie etwas gegen eine Erkältung? *(HAH-ben zee ET-vahs GAY-ghen EYE-nuh air-KEL-toong):* Do you have something for a cold?

In German you speak of taking a medicine "against" (*gegen*) something, not "for" it. You can ask the pharmacist, called *Apotheker(in)*, what he/she recommends to treat your medical condition. If you have a sore throat, a cough, a backache, or some other problem, tell the pharmacist and you'll usually get just what you need.

Können Sie mir etwas gegen Husten geben? KERN-nen zee meer ET-vahs GAY-ghen HOOST-en GAY-ben	Could you give me something for a cough?
Können Sie mir etwas gegen Halsentzündung geben? KERN-nen zee meer ET-vahs GAY-ghen HALLS-ent-TSEWN-doong GAY-ben	Could you give me something for a sore throat?
Haben Sie etwas gegen Muskelkater? HAH-ben zee ET-vahs GAY-ghen MOOS-kel-KAH-ter	Do you have something for sore/stiff muscles?
Haben Sie etwas gegen Sonnenbrand? HAH-ben zee ET-vahs GAY-ghen SON-nen-brahnt	Do you have something for sunburn?

Ich möchte homöopathische Heilmittel probieren. *(eekh MERG-tuh home-er-oh-PAH-tish-uh HYLE-mit-tel pro-BEER-en):* I'd like to try homeopathic remedies.

The two most common forms of alternative or "complementary" medicine in Germany are homeopathy (*die Homöopathie*) and acupuncture (*Akupunktur*). Although acupuncture has its roots in China, the so-called father of homeopathy was the German physician Samuel Hahnemann (1755–1843), who developed the theory and coined the word *homeopathy*. (In 1833, another German named Constantin Hering brought homeopathy to America.)

Controversial from its beginnings in the late eighteenth century, homeopathic treatments or remedies (*Heilmittel*), using natural ingredients, are generally not covered by health insurance in Germany or Switzerland (but are to some extent in Austria). Homeopathic remedies and herbal medicines are largely unregulated in Germany. Most of them can be bought without a prescription at a pharmacy. Many herbal medicines (*Naturheilmittel*), vitamins, dietary supplements, and natural ingredients can be found at a *Reformhaus*, a natural food store that has been a German institution since 1900, and sometimes at a *Bioladen*, an organic food store.

Kennen Sie einen guten Heilpraktiker? KEN-nen zee EYE-nen GOOT-en hyle-PRAHK-tik-er	Do you know of a good nonmedical practitioner?

Wie lange dauert eine Akupunkturbehandlung? *(vee LAHNG-uh DOW-ert EYE-nuh ah-koo-poonk-TOOR-buh-HAHND-loong)*: How long does an acupuncture treatment take?

A typical acupuncture session lasts about twenty to thirty minutes. Certain kinds of acupuncture treatments are covered by German health insurance, but not all. Most of the recognized treatments are for joint or knee pain, and pain associated with the spinal column. Patients must pay out of their own pocket for acupuncture treatments not covered by insurance. In German, an acupuncturist is called an *Akupunkteur(in)* or an *Akupunktur-Arzt/Ärztin* (masculine/feminine).

Kennen Sie einen guten Akupunkteur?	Do you know of a good acupuncturist?
KEN-nen zee EYE-nen GOOT-en ah-koo-poonk-TEWR	

 Ich suche einen Chiropraktiker. *(eekh ZOOKH-uh EYE-nen kee-ro-PRAHK-tee-ker)*: I'm looking for a chiropractor.

Chiropractic was invented by the American Daniel David Palmer (1845–1913). The term *Chiropraktiker* (chiropractor) is not an officially recognized designation in Germany, but it is in Switzerland. (Although the University of Zurich offers a degree in chiropractic, in Germany that is not possible.) A chiropractor in Germany is technically either a *Chirotherapeut* or a *Heilpraktiker*. A German medical doctor (*Arzt/Ärztin*) may use what is called *Chirotherapie* (chiropractic therapy). In most cases chiropractic is covered by insurance, but you may want to ask about coverage.

Mein Rücken/Nacken tut weh.   My back/neck hurts.

myne REWK-ken / NAHK-en

toot vay

Ich habe Schmerzen (hier) in der   I have pain (here) in my spinal

Wirbelsäule.   column.

eekh HAH-buh SHMAIRTS-en (here)

in dare VEER-bel-ZOY-luh

Chapter 14

Communication

 Ich möchte Briefmarken für diesen Brief kaufen. *(eekh MERG-tuh BREEF-mark-en fewr DEE-zen breef KOW-fen):* I'd like to buy stamps for this letter.

The typical German post office, or *das Postamt* (dahs POST-ahmt), today is drastically different from that of just a decade ago. *Die Deutsche Post AG*, while still government owned, is run much more like a business than the staid pre-1995 *Bundespost*. Instead of bureaucratic workers standing behind windows with signs for just one type of service, today you simply go to the next available clerk to buy stamps, send a letter or postcard, ship a package, send a fax, or buy a Western Union money order, or *die Geldanweisung* (dee gelt-ahn-VYE-zoong).

The opening hours (*Öffnungszeiten*) are much better, too. Most German post offices are open from 9:00 A.M. to 6:00 P.M. (09.00–18.00), with an hour off for lunch at smaller offices. Some main post offices and train station or airport offices are open up to twenty-four hours a day and even on Sunday and some holidays. Each post office has its business hours posted at the door. Also see the excellent German post office website (www.deutschepost.de, also in English), where you can buy stamps online and conduct certain other kinds of postal business.

You don't really need to know a lot of German to do business at the post office. If you hand the clerk a letter or postcard addressed to the United States, he or she will know what to do. The price will appear on the cash-register screen, just as it does in a regular store.

Ich möchte drei Briefmarken zu siebzig Cent.	I'd like three seventy-cent stamps.
eekh MERG-tuh dry BREEF-mark-en tsu ZEEB-tsik cent	
Ich möchte Briefmarken für dieses Paket kaufen.	I'd like to buy stamps for this package.
eekh MERG-tuh BREEF-mark-en fewr DEE-zes pahk-ET KOW-fen	
Wie viel kostet eine Briefmarke für eine Postkarte nach...	How much is a stamp for a postcard to . . .
vee feel KOST-et EYE-nuh BREEF-mark-uh fewr EYE-nuh POST-kart-uh nahk	
Bitte mit Luftpost.	By airmail, please.
BIT-tuh mitt LUFT-post	
Wie ist die Postleitzahl für...?	What's the postal code for . . .?
vee ist dee POST-lite-tsahl fewr	

Haben Sie ein Faxgerät? *(HAH-ben zee eyn FAHX-guh-rate):* Do you have a fax machine?

Besides at the post office, you can also send or receive a fax at German FedEx or UPS stores, most office-supply stores (*Bürobedarf*), Internet cafés, or your hotel.

Ich möchte etwas faxen.	I'd like to fax something.
eekh MERG-tuh ET-vas FAHX-en	
Kann ich hier ein Fax empfangen?	Can I receive a fax here?
kahn eekh here eyn fahx	
emp-FAHNG-en	

 Gibt es ein Internetcafé in der Nähe? *(gibt ess eyn in-ter-net-kah-FAY in dare NAY-uh):* Is there an Internet café nearby?

You will find Internet cafés and Wi-Fi locations, called *W-LAN* (vay-lahn), in almost any German town or city. In larger cities they are numerous and easy to find. German Starbucks, McCafés, and other coffee shops also offer wireless Internet access, usually for a fee. Often overlooked Internet resources, especially in larger cities, are public and university libraries, or *die Bibliothek* (dee BIB-lee-oh-tek). Most German hotels also offer Internet access, at prices ranging from free (rare!) to 20 euros or more for twenty-four hours. If you're not using your own computer, the biggest problem is adjusting to the German QWERTZ keyboard and its different layout—with many important keys either missing (no "@" key!) or located in strange places for people used to the U.S. QWERTY keyboard. (You can type "@" but it isn't pretty: press the "Alt Gr" key plus "Q" to make the @ symbol appear.)

Wie viel kostet eine (halbe)   How much does (half) an hour cost?

  Stunde?

vee feel KOST-et EYE-nuh (HAHL-buh)

  SHTOON-duh

Ich möchte meine E-Mails lesen.   I'd like to check my e-mail.

eekh MERG-tuh MY-nuh EE-mails

  LAY-zen

Ich möchte eine E-Mail schicken.   I'd like to send an e-mail.

eekh MERG-tuh EYE-nuh EE-mail

  SHICK-en

Wie ist Ihre E-Mail-Adresse?   What's your e-mail address?

vee ist EAR-uh EE-mail uh-DRESS-uh

 Kann ich meinen eigenen Laptop benutzen? *(kahn eekh MY-nen EYE-guh-nen LAP-top buh-NOOT-sen):* Can I use my own laptop?

If you take your own U.S. laptop to Europe, it will work fine with just a plug adapter. Most modern portable computers and other battery-powered devices (cameras, cell phones, etc.) have built-in voltage adapters or external power adapters that will automatically switch between 110 volts (USA) and 220 volts (Europe).

 Ich möchte telefonieren/anrufen. *(eekh MERG-tuh tel-eh-foh-NEER-en/AHN-roof-en):* I'd like to make a phone call.

Even though it seems that practically every German has a cell phone, or *das Handy* (dahs HAHN-dee), these days, it is still easy to find phone booths, called *Telefonzellen* (tel-uh-fohn-TSELL-en), and public phones. Some German public phones do not take coins. You need a phone card to use them.

If you take your own cell phone to Europe, make sure it is an international GSM multiband version that works with a SIM card. A normal U.S. wireless phone will not work in Europe.

 Ich möchte ein Handy mieten/kaufen. *(eekh MERG-tuh eyn HAHN-dee MEE-ten/KOW-fen)*: I'd like to rent/buy a cell phone.

You can rent a multiband cell phone for short-term use in Germany before or during your trip. But if you travel to Europe on a regular basis, consider buying either a multiband cell phone that works in Germany and the United States, or an inexpensive European cell phone that uses a prepaid SIM card (and is often cheaper than renting). The only disadvantage of a European phone is that you won't know your number until you buy the phone and its SIM card. For business people who want to have their own number wherever they are, a multiband GSM phone may be the best idea. The downside: Calls on a U.S. multiband phone in Europe (local or international, incoming or outgoing) usually cost about a dollar a minute, compared to 15–30 cents per minute for a German prepaid phone.

Darf ich dein/Ihr Telefon/Handy benutzen? darf eekh dyne/ear TEL-eh-fohn/ HAHN-dee buh-NOOT-sen	May I use your phone/cell phone? (familiar/formal)
Am Apparat. ahm AHP-uh-raht	Speaking. (This is he/she speaking.)
Frau/Herr...ist nicht da. frow/hair...ist nikht dah	Ms. or Mrs./Mr. . . . is not in.

**Kann ich ihm/ihr etwas
ausrichten?**
kahn eekh eem/ear ET-vahs
OWS-rikh-ten

Can I take a message for him/her?

**Ich möchte gern Frau/Herrn...
sprechen.**
eekh MERG-tuh gehrn frow/
hairn...SHPREKH-en

I'd like to speak with Ms. or Mrs./Mr. . . .

 Können Sie das bitte wiederholen? *(KERN-nen zee dahs
BIT-tuh VEE-dare-HOHL-en):* Could you please repeat that?

Talking on the phone is often more difficult than face-to-face conversation. Don't be afraid to ask the person on the other end of the line to repeat something. To ask them to speak more slowly, say: *Langsamer
bitte* (LONG-zahm-er BIT-tuh).

**Kann ich eine Nachricht
hinterlassen?**
kahn eekh EYE-nuh NAKH-rikht
HIN-ter-LAHS-sen

Can I leave a message?

Wissen Sie die Vorwahl nach...
WISS-en zee dee FOR-vahl nakh

Do you know the area code for . . .

**Ich habe mich/Sie haben sich
verwählt.**
eekh HAH-buh meekh/zee
HAH-ben zeekh fer-VAYLT

I/You dialed the wrong number.

Bitte, rufen Sie mich an! *(BIT-tuh ROOF-en zee meekh on):* Please give me a call!

This is the formal "you" form of a request. If you're talking to a close friend or relative, you should say, *Bitte, ruf mich an!* (BIT-tuh roof meekh on).

 Smith. *Smith. (your own last name)*

The most common way of answering the phone in German is to simply say your last name. Some Germans, especially the younger generation, answer by saying *Hallo!* (HAHL-lo), just as most Americans would say "Hello?" If you are answering a friend's or relative's phone, you should say *Schmidt bei* (bye) *Jones*, with *Jones* being the last name of your host. To say good-bye when on the phone, say either *Wieder-hören* (VEE-dare-HER-en) or *Tschüs* (chewss). The shorter word is now the more common way to say good-bye in German, on the phone or in person.

Falsch verbunden.	Wrong number.
fallsh fer-BOON-den	
Einen Moment, bitte.	Just a moment, please.
EYE-nen mo-MENT BIT-tuh	

 Kein Anschluss unter dieser Nummer. *(kine ON-shloos OON-ter DEEZ-er NOOM-er):* Not a working number.

If you hear this message on the phone, it usually means you have made a mistake in dialing. If you are dialing outside your area code (*Vor-*

wahlnummer), you must first dial 0 (*null*) and the German area code for the number you're dialing. For instance, if you are in Frankfurt and you want to call someone in Berlin, the phone number (as printed on a business card or a letterhead) would look like this example: 0 30 279 XX XX (of course, a real phone number would have numbers rather than X's). The 30 is the *Vorwahlnummer* for Berlin. If you dial the same number from a phone in Berlin, you would not use the "0 30" part of the number. If you call the Berlin number from outside of Germany, you must add the country code (49) but drop the 0: + 49 30 279 XX XX. German cell phone numbers do not have a city code. They have a three-digit area code like 151, 160, or 172. To call a German cell phone (*das Handy*), use the same procedures previously described. Note: In Germany the caller always pays for a call to a cell phone. The recipient only pays if there are extra long-distance or roaming charges.

German toll-free 0 800 numbers do exist, but they are much rarer in Germany than in the United States. Most German companies do not have toll-free numbers; they typically charge 14 euro cents a minute to call them! Although this shocks most Americans and Canadians, it seems to be the norm in German-speaking countries. It is also possible to call 800 numbers in the United States and Canada from Germany, but the call is not free. Usually, there is an announcement (in German) telling you that the call is not toll-free. This can still be helpful in cases where the only number listed is a North American 800 number.

Chapter 15

Sports

 Wann findet das Fußballspiel statt? *(vahn FIN-det dahs FOOS-ball-shpeel shtahtt):* When is the soccer (football) match?

In Germany, as in Europe and throughout most of the world, the game crowned "King Football," or *König Fußball* (KERN-ig FOOS-ball), is, by far, the top sport of the land. German children grow up playing and watching the game known as *football* in most of the world outside of North America. The professional soccer teams of the German *Bundesliga* (national league) are similar to American football teams (but with less colorful names) and their highly paid players. Germany's *Bundesliga* (Austria also has its own national league) is composed of two divisions: the regular *Bundesliga* and the lower division, called the *Zweite Bundesliga* (second division). At the end of each season, the two bottom teams in the top division are relegated to the second division and replaced by the two top teams in the second division. There is also a third division, plus many regional and amateur clubs all across Germany. Even the smallest towns in Germany have amateur teams with their own soccer fields.

The German professional teams (or clubs) usually take the name of their city or region, although larger cities may have more than one *Bundesliga* club. Some of the best-known teams include Bayer Leverkusen, FC Bayern München (Munich), Hamburger SV, Borussia Dortmund, FC Schalke 04 (Gelsenkirchen, founded in 1904), and Werder Bremen. (The "FC" stands for *Fußballclub,* or soccer club; the "SV" for *Sportverein,* or sports club.) The top *Bundesliga* teams are large successful businesses that pay their top players huge salaries like those earned by top baseball or football players in the United States. German teams often have huge corporate-sponsored stadiums like the 340-million-euro Allianz Arena in Munich that opened in 2005 and seats 66,000 spectators. The city's two pro teams play there, and the stadium was a site for the 2006 World Cup games.

Wie viel kostet der Eintritt?　　　How much is admission?
vee feel KOST-et dare EYN-tritt

 Welche Sportarten mögen Sie? *(VELL-khuh SHPORT-ahr-ten MERG-en zee):* What kind of sports do you like?

Fußball is definitely the number one sport for Germans, but they also enjoy many other types of sporting activities, ranging from handball and auto and horse racing to tennis and volleyball. Although there is an American football league in Germany, the U.S. version plays only a minor role compared to soccer, and most Germans only know about baseball from the movies.

Ich reite gern.　　　I like to ride horseback.
eekh RYE-tuh gehrn

Ich spiele gern Basketball.	I like to play basketball.
eekh SHPEE-luh gehrn BAS-ket-ball	
Ich spiele gern Golf.	I like to play golf.
eekh SHPEE-luh gehrn golf	
Ich spiele gern Volleyball.	I like to play volleyball.
eekh SHPEE-luh gehrn VOL-lee-ball	

 Gibt es einen Badestrand in der Nähe? *(gibt ess EYE-nen BAH-des-shtrahnt in dare NAY-uh):* Is there a bathing beach nearby?

Besides beaches on the Baltic (*die Ostsee*) and the North Sea (*die Nordsee*), there are many public pools (indoor and outdoor), ponds, reservoirs, and lakes for swimming in Germany. In the summer, lakes and ponds are very popular swimming spots.

Gibt es ein Schwimmbad in **der Nähe?**	Is there a swimming pool nearby?
gibt ess eyn SHVIMM-baht in dare NAY-uh	
Ich schwimme gern.	I like to swim.
eekh SHVIM-muh gehrn	

 Gibt es eine Strandwache? *(gibt ess EYE-nuh SHTRAHNT-vahkh-uh):* Is there a (beach) lifeguard on duty?

Bathing beaches and swimming pools in Germany may or may not have a lifeguard on duty. Now you know how to ask about that. At a beach, you may also want to ask:

Kann man hier ohne Gefahr schwimmen?

Is it safe to swim here?

kahn mahn here OH-nuh guh-FAHR SHVIM-men

Wann ist Flut/Ebbe?

When is high tide/low tide?

vahn ist floot/EB-buh

 Ich fahre/laufe gern Ski. *(eekh FAHR-uh/LOW-fuh gehrn shee)*: I like to ski.

In the mountain regions of Germany and in most of Austria, skiing is a very popular winter sport. Alpine skiing and the cross-country relay were first included at the 1936 Winter Olympic Games held in the Bavarian cities of Garmisch and Partenkirchen (although the Games were boycotted by Austrian and Swiss skiers because of a ban on ski instructors, who were considered pros). The Austrian city of Innsbruck played host to both the 1964 and 1976 Winter Olympics. St. Moritz in Switzerland hosted the II Olympic Winter Games in 1928.

Ich möchte einen Liftpass für einen Tag/drei Tage.

I'd like a lift pass for a day/three days.

eekh MERG-tuh EYE-nen LIFT-pahss fewr EYE-nen tahkh/dry TAHG-uh

Können wir eine Skiausrüstung mieten?

Could we rent ski equipment?

KERN-nen veer EYE-nuh SHEE-ows-rewst-oong MEE-ten

Wer ist der Favorit bei der Regatta? *(vehr ist dare FAHV-oh-ritt by dare ray-GAHT-tuh):* Who's the favorite in the regatta?

The *Kieler Woche* (KEEL-er VOKH-uh, "Kiel Week") sailing regatta is the largest sailing event in the world and one of the most prestigious. Held in June in the northern German city of Kiel and the Bay of Kiel (*Kieler Bucht*) on the Baltic Sea (*die Ostsee*), *Kieler Woche* is about much more than water sports. It features competitions in more than thirty sports, including cycling, golf, basketball, bowling, handball, field hockey, rugby, roller-skating, chess, and even a road race for school kids. In addition to the regatta itself, Kiel Week's so-called *Holsten-bummel* claims to be the largest summer festival in northern Europe.

 Ich fahre gern Rad. *(eekh FAHR-uh gehrn raht):* I like bicycling.

Besides being a sport and a good form of exercise, cycling is also a popular way of getting around in German towns and cities. Bike paths, called *Fahrradwege* (FAHR-raht-VAY-guh), are very common (and dangerous for pedestrians who stray into them!). Rush hour in many German towns consists of hordes of people cycling to work or back home.

In larger German towns and resort areas, it is possible to rent bicycles for the day or for longer periods. Look for a sign saying *Fahradvermietung,* or "Bike Rental" in English.

Können wir ein Rad mieten?   Can we rent a bike?
KERN-nen veer eyn raht MEE-ten

131

Wer hat die heutige Etappe gewonnen?
vehr haht dee HOY-tee-guh
AYE-tahp-puh guh-WOHN-nen

Who won today's stage (of the race)?

 Ich wandre gern (in den Bergen). *(eekh VAHN-druh gehrn [in dane BARE-gen]):* I like to hike/go hiking (in the mountains).

Probably the most popular leisure-time family activity in Germany and Austria is hiking, called *das Wandern* (dahs VAHN-dehrn). Germans and other Europeans are lovers of the great outdoors. Many of them think nothing of a weekend or vacation hiking day that covers 15–20 kilometers (10–16 miles) or more.

 Haben Sie einen Tennisplatz frei? *(HAH-ben zee EYE-nen TEN-nis-plahts fry):* Do you have a tennis court available?

In their day, German tennis stars Boris Becker and Steffi Graf helped make tennis an even more popular sport in Germany. Although public tennis courts are still rare, you will find many private and club courts at reasonable rates. Today, German-Swiss champ Michael Federer continues the Germanic tennis tradition.

Ich brauche einen Tennisschläger.
eekh BROW-khuh EYE-nen
TEN-nis-schlay-gher

I need a tennis racket.

Ich möchte ein Autorennen sehen. *(eek MERG-tuh eyn OW-toh-renn-en ZAY-en):* I'd like to see a car race.

Most Germans are much more familiar with Formula One, or *Formel Eins* (FORM-el eynz), than stock car racing. The former German Formula One racing pilot Michael Schumacher and one-time Austrian racer Niki Lauda are national heroes. The famous Nürburgring racetrack in Germany has a long history dating to 1927.

 Können wir zum Basketballspiel gehen? *(KERN-nen veer tsoom BAS-ket-ball-shpeel GAY-en):* Can we go to the basketball game?

Besides soccer, basketball and ice hockey are popular spectator sports in Germany. As with soccer, there is also a *Basketball Bundesliga* (German Basketball League) for professional basketball in Germany, with a total of eighteen teams. Players are predominantly from Germany and the United States.

Ist das ein Auswärtsspiel oder ein Heimspiel?	Is that an away game/match or a home game/match?
ist dahs eyn OWSS-vairts-shpeel oh-dare eyn HYME-shpeel	

 Wo können wir ein Galopprennen sehen? *(voh KERN-nen veer eyn gahl-LOP-REN-nen ZAY-en):* Where can we see a horse race?

There are over forty-five horse-racing tracks, called *Pferderennbahnen* (pfer-duh-RENN-bah-nen), in Germany. On German (and most

Central European) racetracks the horses run in a clockwise direction rather than the counterclockwise direction now common in most countries. (Formula One auto racing is also run clockwise, in imitation of European horse racing, while NASCAR races go counterclockwise.) The best-known horse-racing tracks in Germany are in Baden-Baden (Iffezheim), Berlin-Hoppegarten, Düsseldorf, Hamburg-Horn (site of the German Derby in July, Germany's biggest race), and Munich. There is also harness racing (*Trabrennen*), with or without a sulky (two-wheeled cart), in Germany and Austria.

Chapter 16

Friendship and Romance

 Woher kommst du/kommen Sie? *(voh-HARE kohmst doo/ KOHM-men zee)*: Where are you from? (familiar/formal)

German, like every language, has standard phrases and expressions used when you meet people and get acquainted. How do you go beyond "Hi, how are you?" and basic conversation? How do you make friends? What if friendship turns into romance?

Ich komme aus...   I come from . . .

eekh KOHM-muh ows

 Was sind Sie von Beruf? *(vahs zint zee fonn buh-ROOF)*: What is your occupation?

Germans are more reserved about talking about their private life, including their job, but there are times when it is appropriate to ask this question. Before you are asked the same question, learn the German term for your own job or profession. Notice that German usually does not use *ein* or *eine* (*a, an*) in the answer:

Ich bin Lehrer/Lehrerin.   I'm a teacher. (male/female)
eekh bin LEHR-er/LEHR-er-in

Ich arbeite bei einer Bank.   I work for a bank.
eekh AR-by-tuh by EYE-ner bahnk

Ich bin Student/Studentin.   I'm a (college) student. (male/female)
eekh bin shtoo-DENT/shtoo-DENT-in

Ich bin pensioniert.   I'm retired.
eekh bin pen-see-oh-NEERT

 Wo wohnst du/wohnen Sie? *(voh vohnst doo/VOH-nen zee)*: Where do you live? (familiar/formal)

To answer this question you can say:

Ich wohne in _____.   I live in _____.
eekh VOH-nuh in   (city/town)

Ich wohne auf dem Land.   I live in the country.
eekh VOH-nuh owf dame lahnt

Ich habe ein Haus/eine Wohnung.   I have a house/an apartment.
eekh HAH-buh EYN house/EYE-nuh
    VOH-noong

 Was hast du heute vor? *(vahs hahst doo HOY-tuh for)*: What are your plans today? (familiar)

If you are not yet on familiar (*du*) terms, you would ask:

Was haben Sie heute vor?   What are your plans today? (formal)
vahs HAH-ben zee HOY-tuh for

Möchten Sie mit mir essen gehen/Kaffee trinken gehen?
(MERG-ten zee mitt meer ESS-en GAY-en/kah-FAY TRINK-en GAY-en): Would you like to go eat something/have coffee with me?

If you would like to ask someone out, here are some more phrases you could use:

Willst du einen Film sehen?	Do you want to see a movie?
villst doo EYE-nen film ZAY-en	
Gehen wir zum Mittagessen.	Let's go have lunch.
GAY-en veer tsoom MIT-takh-ESS-en	
Hast du ein Lieblingsrestaurant?	Do you have a favorite restaurant?
hahst doo eyn LEEB-lings-REST-ow-rahnt	

 Du bist sehr nett. *(doo bist zehr nett):* You are very nice.

If there is some good chemistry between you and that certain other person, you are probably now on *du* terms and you may need more "familiar" phrases like these:

Du bist (sehr) schön!	You're (very) beautiful!
doo bist zehr shern	
Du bist so hübsch.	You're so cute/handsome.
doo bist so hewbsh	
Du bist so charmant.	You are so charming.
doo bist zo shar-MAHNT	

Du machst mich so glücklich, mein Schatz! *(doo mahkhs meekh zo GLEW-likh mine shahts)*: You make me so happy, my darling!

The most popular German pet name, or *Kosename* (KOH-zuh-NAHM-uh), is *Schatz* (shahts) for "treasure" or "dear," which has many variations: *Schatzi, Schätzchen, Schätzelchen, Schätzlein*, etc. Other German words of endearment are: *Bärchen* (little bear), *Biene* (bee), *Engel* (angel), *Gummibärchen* (gummy bear), *Hasi* (bunny), *Herz* (heart), *Honigbienchen* (honeybee), *Knuddel* (cuddles), *Kuschelbär* (cuddle bear), *Liebling* (darling), *Mausi* (little mouse), *Schnuckiputzi* (sweetie pie), *Spatzi* (little sparrow), and *Zaubermaus* (enchanting mouse).

Ohne dich kann ich nicht leben.   I can't live without you.
OH-nuh deekh kahn eekh nikht
   LAY-ben

 Können wir uns wiedersehen? *(KERN-nen veer oonz VEE-der-ZAY-en)*: Could we see each other again?

If the relationship seems to be progressing well, you can ask about getting together again later. To be more specific, you may want to say:

Wo und wann kann ich dich   Where and when can I see you again?
   wiedersehen?
voh oont vahn kahn eekh deekh
   VEE-der-ZAY-en

Ich kann kaum warten bis ich dich wiedersehe.	I can hardly wait to see you again.
eekh kahn kowm VAHR-ten bis eekh deekh VEE-der-ZAY-uh	
Ich werde dich vermissen.	I'm going to miss you.
eekh VEHR-duh deekh fer-MISS-en	

 Ich liebe dich. *(eekh LEE-buh deekh):* I love you.

If you're sure it's love, then this is the right phrase. If you're not ready to go quite that far, you may want to use these somewhat milder phrases:

Ich hab dich lieb.	I'm very fond of you.
eekh hahb deekh leep	
Ich mag dich sehr.	I like you a lot.
eekh mag deekh zehr	

 Du bist ein Schatz. *(doo bist eyn shahts):* You're a dear.

Romantic conversation requires the special German language of love. Review the other popular German terms of endearment given previously, and you can insert any of those to replace *Schatz* in this sentence.

Chapter 17

Numbers, the Calendar, and Time

 Welchen Tag haben wir heute? *(VELKH-en tahg HAH-ben veer HOY-tuh)*: What day is today?

The German and European calendar, or *der Kalender* (dare kah-LEN-dare), starts the week with Monday (*Montag*) and shows the two weekend days together. The days of the week in German often resemble English (here shown with the standard German abbreviation for each day). In northern Germany, the word *Sonnabend* (SONN-ah-bent) for "Sunday eve" is often used for Saturday instead of *Samstag*.

Montag (Mo)   Monday
MOHN-tahg
Dienstag (Di)   Tuesday
DEENS-tahg
Mittwoch (Mi)   Wednesday
MITT-vokh

Donnerstag (Do)	Thursday
DON-ners-tahg	
Freitag (Fr)	Friday
FRY-tahg	
Samstag (Sa)	Saturday
SAHMS-tahg	
Sonntag (So)	Sunday
SONN-tahg	
Heute ist Montag.	Today is Monday.
HOY-tuh ist MOHN-tahg	

Im Juni fliegen wir nach Berlin. *(im YOO-nee FLEE-ghen veer nahkh bare-LEEN):* In June we're flying to Berlin.

Like the days of the week, the months of the year, or *Monate* (MOH-naht-uh), in German are also fairly similar to (or the same as) English. To say "in June" or "in March" you say *im Juni* (im YOO-nee) or *im März* (im mehrts). German uses *im* for "in" with the months. All the months are masculine (*der*).

Januar	January
YAHN-ooh-ahr	
Februar	February
FEHB-rooh-ahr	
März	March
mehrts	
April	April
ah-PRILL	

Mai mye	May
Juni YOO-nee	June
Juli YOO-lee	July
August ow-GOOST	August
September zep-TEM-ber	September
Oktober ok-TOH-ber	October
November no-VEM-ber	November
Dezember day-TSEM-ber	December
Er ist im März wieder da. air ist im mehrts VEE-der dah	He'll be back in March.

 Er kommt am 4. Mai an. *(air kohmt ahm FEER-ten mye ahn):* He arrives on May 4.

German and European dates are given in the logical, progressive order of day, month, year. Thus the numerical date of 03.10.09 (as written in German) is the third day of October 2009. (October 3 happens to be the German national holiday, *Tag der Deutschen Einheit*, or German Unity Day.) To express "on October third," you would say *am dritten Oktober* (ahm DRIT-ten ohk-TOH-ber). This formula is used for any date in German. (See the following for more about the ordinal numbers used in dates.)

 Das Konzert findet im Herbst statt. *(dahs KOHN-tsert FIN-det im hairbst shtaht):* The concert takes place in the fall.

As with the months, use *im* to say "in" a season: *im Sommer* (in the summer). The four seasons—all masculine (*der*)—in German are:

Frühling	spring
FREW-ling	
Sommer	summer
SOM-mer	
Herbst	fall
hairbst	
Winter	winter
VIN-ter	

 Wir haben drei Kinder, zwei Töchter und einen Sohn. *(veer HAH-ben dry KIN-der tsvye TERKH-ter oont EYE-nen zohn):* We have three children; two daughters and a son.

In order to use basic numbers and to understand and use dates and time in German, you should have at least an elementary command of German numbers.

null	0
nool	
eins	1
eyns	

zwei	2
tsvye	
drei	3
dry	
vier	4
feer	
fünf	5
fewnf	
sechs	6
zex	
sieben	7
ZEE-ben	
acht	8
ahkt	
neun	9
noyn	
zehn	10
tsayn	
elf	11
elf	
zwölf	12
tsverlf	

 Wir fahren am siebten Mai ab. *(veer FAHR-en ahm ZEEP-ten mye ahb):* We depart on the seventh of May.

The German equivalent of the English *-th* ending for ordinal numbers is *-te* or *-ten*: *der zehnte Mai* (the tenth of May), *am zehnten Mai* (on May 10th). To form an ordinal number in German, you simply add the *-te* or *-ten* ending (which one depends on the grammatical case) to any cardinal number smaller than 20: *vier* + *te* = *vierte* (four + th = fourth), except for the few following exceptions:

erste	first
AIR-stuh	
dritte	third
DRIT-tuh	
siebte	seventh
ZEEP-tuh	
Am einundzwanzigsten Januar (am 21. Januar)	on January 21st
ahm eyn-oont-TSVANT-sig-sten	
Bis zum 3. (dritten) November	by/until November 3rd
bis tsoom DRIT-ten no-VEM-ber	
Sein Büro ist die zweite Tür links.	His office is the second door on the left.
zyn bew-ROH ist dee TSVY-tuh tewr linx	
Der erste Zug fährt heute um 14 Uhr ab.	The first train leaves at 2:00 P.M. today.
dare ERST-uh tsook fairt HOY-tuh oom FEER-tsayn oohr ahp	

 Wie viel Uhr ist es? *(vee feel oohr ist ess):* What time is it?

Another common way to ask the time in German is: *Wie spät ist es?* (vee shpate ist ess), or *How late is it?* To answer this question in daily conversation, German-speakers use the same twelve-hour time that is used in English, but the use of twenty-four-hour time ("military time") is much more common in German and is always used for schedules (TV, rail, airline, etc.), store hours, appointments, or for any situation where it is important to be clear about the time. The following are some common standard phrases used when talking about time informally:

Es ist...Uhr.	It is . . . o'clock.
ess ist...oohr	
Es ist elf Uhr.	It is eleven o'clock.
ess ist elf oohr	
Es ist elf Uhr zwanzig.	It is eleven twenty.
ess ist elf oohr TSVAHN-tsikh	
Es ist Viertel zehn.	It is nine fifteen.
ess ist FEER-tel tsayn	
Es ist Dreiviertel zehn.	It is a quarter to ten.
es ist dry-FEER-tel tsayn	

 Es ist halb zehn. *(ess ist halp tsayn):* It's nine thirty. (literally, "halfway to 10:00")

When telling time in German, think of the hourglass as being half full, not half empty. For instance, 5:30 is halfway to 6:00, so you say *halb sechs* (halp zex). *Halb* is not used with twenty-four-hour time, however: *Es ist zweiundzwanzig Uhr dreißig* (22:30).

Es ist halb zwei.	It's one thirty. (halfway to 2:00)
ess ist halp tsvye	
Ich möchte die Nachrichten um	I'd like to see the news at 8:00 P.M.
zwanzig Uhr (20.00) sehen.	
eekh MERG-tuh dee NAHKH-rikh-ten	
oom TSVAHN-tsikh oohr zay-en	

Sein Flug kommt um neunzehn
Uhr zehn (19.10) an.

His flight arrives at 7:10 P.M.

zyne floog kommt oom NOYN-tsayn
oohr tsayn ahn

 Es ist Viertel nach zehn./Es ist Viertel elf. *(ess ist FEER-tel nahk tsayn/ess ist FEER-tel elf)*: It's a quarter past ten. (10:15)

This is another German clock-time format. Similar to *halb* (half), the "quarter" phrases can be used without any preposition (*Viertel elf*), but unlike *halb*, they can also be used with *vor* or *nach*, as shown here.

Es ist Viertel vor zehn./Es ist
Dreiviertel zehn.

It's quarter to ten. (9:45)

ess ist FEER-tel for tsayn/es ist
dry-FEER-tel tsayn

Es ist zehn nach zwei.

It is ten past two. (2:10)

ess ist tsayn nahkh tsvye

Es ist fünf (Minuten) vor vier.

It is five (minutes) to four. (3:55)

ess ist fewnf (mee-NOO-ten) for feer

 Wann treffen wir uns? *(vahn TREF-fen veer oons)*: When should we meet?

Will we be meeting today (*heute*), tomorrow (*morgen*), next week (*nächste Woche*), or the day after tomorrow (*übermorgen*)? Here are some helpful German "time" words and phrases:

gestern GHES-tern	yesterday
heute HOY-tuh	today
jetzt yetst	now
morgen MOHR-ghen	tomorrow
übermorgen EW-ber-MOHR-ghen	day after tomorrow
vorgestern FOR-ghes-tern	day before yesterday

**Ich kann Sie/dich morgen um
    14 Uhr treffen.**
eek kahn zee/deekh MOHR-ghen
    oom FEER-tsayn oohr TREF-fen
	I can meet you (formal/familiar)
	    tomorrow at 2:00 P.M.

 Wir treffen uns nächste Woche. *(veer TREF-fen oons NEX-tuh VOHK-uh):* We're meeting next week.

The following are more phrases you can use when talking about future events:

**Können wir uns am Montag
    treffen?**
KERN-nen veer oons ahm
    MOHN-tahg TREF-fen
	Could we meet on Monday?

Sie kommen nächsten Monat. zee KOHM-men NEX-ten MOH-naht	They're coming next month.

...nächstes Jahr   . . . next year

NEX-tes yahr

...in einer Woche   . . . in a week

in EYE-ner VOHK-uh

...in vierzehn Tagen   . . . in two weeks (literally, "fourteen
                                         days")

in FEER-tsayn TAHG-en

...in einem Monat   . . . in a month

in EYE-nem MOH-naht

Chapter 18

Weather

 Wie ist das Wetter heute? (*vee ist dahs VET-ter HOY-tuh*): What's the weather like today?

Everybody talks about the weather. (*Alle reden vom Wetter.*) That, of course, includes Austrians, Germans, and the Swiss. It can be very helpful for travelers to know at least some of the more common weather terms in German. Do you want to go hiking or to a museum tomorrow? The weather forecast (*die Wettervorhersage*) may help you decide. Do you need an umbrella (*einen Regenschirm*, eye-nen RAY-ghen-shirm), or not?

Die Sonne scheint.	The sun is shining.
dee SON-nuh shynt	
Es ist (leicht) bewölkt.	It is (partly) cloudy/overcast.
ess ist (lykht) beh-VERLKT	
Es ist (zu) kalt/warm.	It is (too) cold/warm.
ess ist tsoo kahlt/varm	

Es ist schwül.   It's muggy (humid).
ess ist shvewl

Es ist (sehr) windig.   It is (very) windy.
ess ist (zehr) VIN-dig

 Es ist neblig. *(ess ist NAY-blig):* It is foggy.

Many regions of German-speaking Europe are fog-prone at certain times of the year, in addition to experiencing the usual vagaries of weather.

Der Nebel ist sehr dick.   The fog is very thick.
dare NAY-bel ist zehr dick

Es ist stürmisch.   It is stormy (windy).
ess ist STEWRM-ish

Es regnet/schneit.   It is raining/snowing.
ess RAYG-net/SHNYTE

Es blitzt.   There's lightning.
ess blitst

Es hagelt.   It's hailing.
ess HAHG-elt

 Haben Sie den Wetterbericht gehört/gesehen? *(HAH-ben zee dane VET-ter-buh-RICHT guh-HERT/guh-ZAY-en):* Have you heard/seen the weather report?

Der Deutsche Wetterdienst, or *DWD* (German Weather Service), with headquarters in Offenbach, Germany (near Frankfurt am Main), and regional centers in various German cities, provides daily and long-range weather forecasts that are printed in newspapers, published online (www.dwd.de), and broadcast on radio and TV. The DWD also carries out climate studies, and issues pollen reports and severe weather warnings.

 Wie wird das Wetter? *(vee virt dahs VET-ter):* What's the weather going to be like?

Knowing a little German weather vocabulary, the days of the week, and the German numbers (see Chapter 17), it is possible to get the gist of a weather forecast in German.

Wie heißt die Wettervorhersage? vee HYST dee VET-ter-for-HARE-zahg-uh	What's the weather forecast?
Es bleibt schön. ess BLYBT shern	It's going to stay nice.
Es bleibt kalt/warm. ess BLYBT kahlt/varm	It's going to stay cold/warm.
Es wird regnen. ess veert RAYG-nen	It's going to rain.
Regen wird vorausgesagt. RAY-ghen wirt for-OWS-guh-SAHGT	They're forecasting rain.
Einzelne Gewitter werden vorausgesagt. EYN-tsel-nuh guh-VIT-ter VEHR-den for-OWS-guh-SAHGT	They're forecasting scattered thunderstorms.
Das Barometer steigt/fällt. dahs BAR-oh-may-ter stygt/felt	The barometer is climbing/falling.

Es gibt ein Hoch/Tief über Deutschland. ess gibt eyn hoke/teef EW-ber DOYSHT-lahnt	There's a high/low over Germany.
Es wird kalt/warm. ess veert kahlt/varm	It's going to turn cold/warm.
Wir bekommen... veer buh-KOHM-men	We're going to have . . .
...ein Gewitter. eyn guh-VIT-ter	. . . a thunderstorm.
...schönes Wetter. SHERN-es VET-ter	. . . nice weather.
...schlechtes Wetter. SHLEKH-tes VET-ter	. . . bad weather.
...wechselhaftes Wetter. VEX-el-hahf-tes VET-ter	. . . changeable weather.

 Mir ist (es) kalt/warm. *(meer ist [ess] kahlt/vahrm):* I'm cold/warm. (It feels cold/warm to me.)

Warning! If you want to say that you are cold, warm, or hot in German, be careful! You may get odd stares or laughter if you say, for instance, *Ich bin warm.* You just told everyone you're gay. On the other hand, *Ich bin kalt* means you are a cold person or even frigid. *Ich bin heiß* means something like "I'm in heat." The key word you need to add is *mir* (meer), or "to me": *Mir ist (es) kalt.* (To me it is/feels cold.) Adding the pronoun also applies when asking questions. Note that Germans tend to use *warm* to express either "warm" or "hot."

Ich friere. eekh FREER-uh	I'm freezing. (I'm cold.)

154

Nein, mir ist es sehr angenehm. No, it seems quite pleasant to me.
nyne meer ist ess zehr
  AHN-guh-name

Ist (es) dir/Ihnen kalt? Are you cold? (familiar/formal)
ist (ess) deer/EEN-nen kahlt

Ist (es) dir/Ihnen warm? Are you warm/hot? (familiar/formal)
ist (ess) deer/EEN-nen varm

 Wie viel Grad haben wir? *(vee feel graht HAH-ben veer):*
What's the temperature?

The United States is one of the few countries left in the world that use the temperature scale invented by the German physicist Daniel Gabriel Fahrenheit (1686–1736) around 1724. Europeans and the rest of the world use the Celsius (centigrade) scale named for the Swedish astronomer Anders Celsius (1701–1744).

You may already know the standard formula for converting a Celsius temperature to Fahrenheit ($\frac{9}{5} \times C + 32 = F$), but there's a much simpler shortcut formula that you can do in your head. It only gives you a ballpark figure, but at least you will know the approximate temperature. Take the Celsius temperature (for example, 20°) and double it. In this case, that's 40. Then add 30, which gives you 70°F. It's not an exact figure, but it is very close to the actual temperature of 68°F that you would get by using the $\frac{9}{5}$ formula. It works even better with slightly lower temperatures.

You can also learn a few standard Celsius temperatures as a guide: the freezing point of water (0°C/32°F), normal body temperature (37°C/98.6°F), room temperature (20°C/68°F), boiling point of water (100°C/212°F), etc.

Es ist 20 (zwanzig) Grad. It is 20 degrees. (68°F)
ess ist TSVAHN-tsik graht

Es ist 32 (zweiundreißig) Grad. It is 32 degrees. (90°F)
ess ist TSVY-oont-DRY-sik graht

Es ist 0 (null) Grad. It is 0 degrees. (32°F)
ess ist nool graht

Es ist minus 5 (fünf) Grad. It is minus 5 degrees. (23°F)
ess ist MEEN-oos fewnf graht

Es ist 10 (zehn) unter 0 (null). It is 10 below 0. (14°F)
ess ist tsayn OON-ter nool

Es regnet in Strömen. *(ess RAYG-net in STRERM-en):* It's raining cats and dogs. (literally, "in streams/torrents")

Here are a few more typical German weather expressions:

Alle reden vom Wetter, aber Everybody talks about the weather,
   keiner tut etwas dagegen.   but nobody ever does anything
ALL-uh RAY-den fom VET-ter AH-   about it.
   ber KINE-er toot ET-vahs
   dah-GAY-gen

Es war wie ein Blitz aus heiterem It was like a bolt out of the blue.
   Himmel.
ess vahr vee eyn blits ows
   HYE-ter-em HIM-mel

Das ist Schnee von gestern. That's old news. (literally, "yesterday's
dahs ist shnay fon GHES-tern   snow")

Chapter 19

Celebrations and Holidays

 Alles Gute zum Geburtstag! *(ALL-es GOO-tuh tsoom guh-BOORTS-tahg)*: Happy birthday!

If you're lucky enough to be invited to a German birthday party (*Geburtstagsparty*), you can wish the birthday person *Alles Gute zum Geburtstag*, but don't be surprised if the guests begin singing "Happy Birthday" in English. The English version of the song is the most common birthday song in Germany. If you bring a gift, remember that it is *ein Geschenk* (a gift/present) and not *das Gift* (poison)!

Wann hast du/haben Sie Geburtstag?	When is your birthday? (familiar/ formal)
vahn hahst doo/HAH-ben zee guh-BOORTS-tahk	
Ich habe ein Geschenk für dich.	I have a gift for you.
eekh HAH-buh eyn guh-SHENK fewr deekh	

Ich habe eine Karte für dich.   I have a card for you.
eekh HAH-buh EYE-nuh KAR-tuh
  fewr deekh

 Wann findet Oktoberfest statt? *(vahn FIN-det ohk-TOH-ber-fest shtat):* When does Oktoberfest take place?

Don't let the name of the world's biggest fair fool you. Although it always ends in early October, Munich's Oktoberfest begins in late September. Germany's famous beer-and-sausage festival began as a wedding celebration in 1810. The big party at that time was for Bavarian Crown Prince Ludwig and his bride, Princess Therese. The princess gave the Oktoberfest fairground its name: *die Theresienwiese* (Therese's meadow), known by locals as *die Wiesn. Ich geh' auf die Wiesn* is another way of saying, "I'm going to Oktoberfest." At noon on opening day, Munich's mayor, accompanied by the Bavarian governor (*Ministerpräsident*), does the ceremonial tapping of the first keg of Oktoberfest beer with the traditional cry of *O'zapft is!* (It is tapped!) Although beer is definitely king, Oktoberfest is really like a big state fair with carnival rides, Ferris wheels, sideshows, and other attractions for kids. There is also a special "family day" (*Familientag*) during every Oktoberfest that is designed to be less "rowdy" and better suited to bringing the children along.

If you're more of a wine fan, don't miss the world's biggest wine festival in the world, also in September, held farther north in the German state of Rhineland-Palatinate (*Rheinland-Pfalz*). The *Wurstmarkt* (sausage market) in Bad Dürkheim began in the twelfth century, making it much older than Oktoberfest. With a fairlike setting similar to Oktoberfest, visitors can sample over 150 different wines at the *Dürkheimer Wurstmarkt* (DEWRK-hye-mer VOORST-markt).

Ich möchte ein Glas Weißwein/   I'd like a glass of white/red wine.
Rotwein.
eekh MERG-tuh eyn glahs VICE-vine /
   ROHT-vine

 Ist das Bierzelt voll? *(ist dahs BEER-tselt foll):* Is the beer tent full?

Oktoberfest features fourteen giant beer tents (*Bierzelte*) or beer halls (*Bierhallen*). Although some of the six brewer-sponsored halls and the other halls are more popular than others, they all fill up quickly, especially in the evening, despite having combined seating for about 100,000 guests.

 Wo kann ich ein Dirndl kaufen? *(voh kahn eekh eyn DIRN-del KOW-fen):* Where can I buy a dirndl?

The *Dirndlkleid* (DIRN-del-klite), or dirndl dress—just *Dirndl* for short —is the traditional costume worn by women and girls in Bavaria and Austria. Seen at events like Oktoberfest and other traditional celebrations, the *Dirndl* is still popular today, especially for festive occasions. A good dirndl can be expensive, but if you shop around, you may find a good deal at a department store or clothing store in southern Germany or Austria. The men's equivalent is a *Trachtenanzug* (TRAHKH-ten-AHN-tsookh), the Bavarian/Austrian loden (wool) suit; or a *Lederhose* (LAY-dare-HOE-zuh) if the weather isn't too cool.

Kölle Alaaf! *(KERL-luh ah-LAAHF):* A Carnival greeting in Cologne.

The German version of Mardi Gras or Carnival is known as *Fasching* or *Karneval*. But these two main German terms for Carnival also reflect two different kinds of celebrations. Although they are similar and both feature parades and costumes, *Fasching*, as the celebration is known in Bavaria and Austria, has its big day on "Fat Tuesday" (Mardi Gras), also known as Shrove Tuesday. In the Catholic regions of northern Germany (mostly in Cologne and the Rhineland), *Karneval* has its climax a day sooner, on Rose Monday (*Rosenmontag*). The big parades (*Umzüge*) for *Karneval* are on *Rosenmontag*, and the parades in the Rhineland are broadcast on German TV, just like the Macy's Thanksgiving Day parade in New York City. In the south, the parades happen the next day, on *Faschingsdienstag*. Although Cologne/Mainz and Munich are Germany's two main Carnival cities, similar if smaller events are held in many other towns and cities. Even in mainly Protestant Berlin, there is a modest *Karneval* parade. Just like Carnival in Rio or Mardi Gras in New Orleans, the celebration in German-speaking countries is the traditional big blast leading up to Ash Wednesday (*Aschermittwoch*) and the Lenten season that ends on Easter Sunday and used to feature strict fasting, the root word in both *Fasching* and *Fastenzeit* (Lent). Additional common Carnival yells/expressions are:

Helau!   in Düsseldorf
hay-LOW

Ho narro!   in Stuttgart
ho NAR-ro

Hajo!   in Heidelberg
hi-YO

Wir wollen zum Walpurgisnachtfest in Bacharach am Rhein. *(veer VOLL-en tsoom VAHL-poor-ghes-nahkht-fest in BACH-ah-rach ahm rine)*: We want to go to the Walpurgis Night Festival in Bacharach on the Rhine.

Walpurgisnacht (Walpurgis Night, April 30) is a Christian/pagan observance that gets its name from Saint Walburga, or Walpurga (*die Heilige Walpurga*), a woman born in what is now England in 710. Walpurgis Night is a kind of Germanic Halloween, but celebrated in the spring. Saint Walburga traveled to Germany and became a nun at the convent of Heidenheim in Württemberg.

Although the tradition is older, its observance in Germany in modern times was made popular in the 19th century by references to it in Johann Wolfgang von Goethe's drama *Faust*. In *Faust*, the Brocken, the highest peak in the Harz Mountains, is the focal point of *Walpurgisnacht*, and today the Brocken is still one of the biggest sites for the celebration. However, Walpurgis Night parties and festivities take place all across Germany. Many communities organize parties for families and children (à la Halloween), with bonfires, games, and costumes, while on the Rhine there are dances, parties, and fireworks over the water.

 Fröhliche Weihnachten! *(FRER-lee-khuh VYE-nahkh-ten)*: Merry Christmas!

Many of the world's Christmas customs come from Germany and Austria. The Christmas tree, or *der Tannenbaum* (dare TAHN-nen-BOWM), originated in Germany. "Silent Night," or *Stille Nacht* (SHTIL-uh nahkht), was composed in Oberndorf, Austria, and first performed with German lyrics and guitar accompaniment on Christmas Eve in 1818. This world-famous Christmas carol has since been translated into countless other languages.

The most important time in the Christmas celebration for most families in German-speaking Europe is Christmas Eve, or *Heiligabend* (HYE-leekh-AH-bent), when family and friends enjoy *die Bescherung* (beh-SHER-oong), an exchange of gifts, while gathered around the Christmas tree. As in much of Europe, pond-raised carp (*Karpfen*) or roast goose (*Gänsebraten*) is the traditional German Christmas dinner, but turkey is also increasingly popular.

Ein frohes Fest!	Merry Christmas!
eyn FROH-es fest	
Frohe Weihnachten!	Merry Christmas!
FROH-uh VYE-nahkh-ten	

 Prosit Neujahr! *(PRO-sit NOY-yahr):* Happy New Year!

New Year's Eve (*Silvester*) in Germany is the one time of the year when Germans can legally buy and use fireworks. Even before midnight, the skies in larger cities are filled with amateur fireworks of all kinds. In big cities there is also a traditional professional fireworks display.

If you happen to be in Germany around New Year's Day, you may get to see firsthand a bizarre German New Year's custom: "Dinner for One"! This fifteen-minute comedy sketch by two British actors (in English!), recorded in the 1960s in black-and-white, is traditionally broadcast on German television at the end of each year. Its English catchphrase, "The same procedure as every year, James," is familiar to virtually every German.

Alles Gute im neuen Jahr!
ALL-es GOO-tuh im NOY-en yahr

Best wishes for the New Year!

Einen guten Rutsch!
EYE-nen GOO-ten rootsh

Happy New Year! (literally, "A good slide" into the new year!)

 Wo finde ich eine evangelische/katholische Kirche? *(voh FIN-duh eekh EYE-nuh ay-van-GHEL-ish-uh/kah-TOHL-ish-uh KEERKH-uh):* Where can I find a Protestant/Catholic church?

The average rate of church attendance in Europe and the German-speaking countries is much lower than in the United States, but Germany is about evenly split between Catholics and Protestants (Lutheran), with the two confessions having about 25 million members each. There are also minority religions, and even mosques and synagogues in Germany. (There are over three million Muslims in Germany, most of Turkish descent.) While Switzerland is also about half Catholic and half Protestant (with a small percentage of minority religions), Austria and the German state of Bavaria (*Bayern*) are predominantly Roman Catholic (*römisch-katholisch*).

The German terms *evangelisch* (ay-vahn-GHEL-ish) and *katholisch* (kah-TOHL-ish) refer to the Protestant and Catholic religions, respectively. The German leader of the Reformation, Martin Luther (1483–1546), gave his name to the Lutheran faith professed by most of Germany's Protestants. But both the Roman Catholic and Protestant churches in Germany have each lost about five million members since 1990. Church membership in former East Germany is much lower than in the western parts of Germany. About one in three Germans claims membership in no church, sometimes for tax reasons. There is no official state church in Germany, but the government collects a church tax (*Kirchensteuer*, KEERKH-en-stoy-er) of 8 to 9 percent of one's income for the Catholic and Protestant churches and some Jewish congregations (*Kultussteuer*).

Non-Lutheran Protestant denominations such as Baptists, Methodists, Mormons, and Jehovah's Witnesses are generally considered cults or sects (*Sekten*) in Germany, and thus receive no government financial support. The same is true, financially, for Muslims. The planned construction of a large mosque in predominantly Catholic Cologne (*Köln*), home to Germany's tallest cathedral, has stirred up much controversy, which also reflects Germany's failure to better integrate its large Turkish minority population.

The Church of Scientology, which has offices in Berlin and some other German cities, is particularly unpopular in Germany, having actually been verbally attacked by government officials and condemned in print by the authors of several German-language anti-Scientology books.

Wo finde ich eine Moschee? Where can I find a mosque?
voh FIN-duh eekh EYE-nuh mo-SHAY

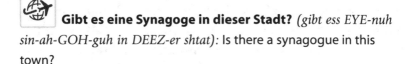 **Gibt es eine Synagoge in dieser Stadt?** (*gibt ess EYE-nuh sin-ah-GOH-guh in DEEZ-er shtat*): Is there a synagogue in this town?

The renovated and restored Jewish synagogue on Oranienburger Straße in Berlin and the newly constructed Ohel Jakob synagogue in Munich are symbols of the return of Jewish life and culture to Germany. Today there are an estimated 200,000 Jews living in Germany, many of them from the former German territories of Eastern Europe and the former Soviet Union. That is only about half of the estimated 400,000 Jews living in Germany prior to 1933 and the rise of the Nazi government. Despite Germany's horrible history in connection with Jews, the nation continues to try to come to terms with its past and find reconciliation. Relations between Germany and Israel are generally good today. Despite neo-Nazi activities (also a problem in many other countries), the vast majority of Germans today are opposed to such antiforeigner, anti-Semitic views.

The Right Phrase for Every Situation...Every Time.